Adrienne :

Blessing
Wishes

[signature] 7/19/13

Alzheimer's
The Identity Thief of the
21st Century

By Robert B. Schaefer

PublishAmerica
Baltimore

This publication contains the opinions and ideas of its author. Author intends to offer information of a general nature. Neither the author nor the publisher are engaged in rendering medical, health or any other kind of personal professional services to the reader. The reader should consult his or her own physician before relying on any information set forth in or implied from this publication. Any reliance on the information herein is at the reader's own discretion.

The author and publisher specifically disclaim all responsibility for any liability, loss, or right, personal or otherwise, which is incurred as a consequence, directly or indirectly, of the use and application of any contents of this book. They further make no representations or warranties with respect to the accuracy or completeness of the contents of this work and specifically disclaim all warranties including without limitation any implied warranty of fitness for a particular purpose. Any recommendations are made without any guarantee on the part of the author or the publisher.

PublishAmerica has allowed this work to remain exactly as the author intended, verbatim, without editorial input.

Hardcover 978-1-4512-1237-2
Softcover 978-1-4512-1344-7
PUBLISHED BY PUBLISHAMERICA, LLLP
www.publishamerica.com
Baltimore

Printed in the United States of America

The highlight of the book for me is the author's very matter-of-fact approach in journaling the devastating trail of Alzheimer's disease, and how this disease process has altered not only his dear wife, Sarah, but also the entire family tapestry. The author focuses a great deal on the communication process, and how well 'keeping it simple' works in caring for Sarah. Communication is the foundation of all of our care, and most especially in caring for persons with dementia, it is critical that we understand this individual may no longer communicate with words, but with feelings. Family and professional care partners will discover many communication strategies in reading this book. Alzheimer's is a dehumanizing condition that robs the person of their dignity and personhood. In this book, readers will discover that the author lifts the disease and focuses on Sarah. Her personhood is alive and well. In fact, when I visited Sarah at Lucy Corr in 2008, Robert and Sarah were dancing. He was humming the tune and she was moving her feet to the music.

Gwendolyn de Geest, educator and author: The Living Dementia Case-Study Approach, Vancouver, Canada.

This book is aptly titled as it was Alzheimer's—The Identity Thief of the 21st Century for Bob Schaefer to share his heart-wrenching journey of caring for Sarah. This book offers families and health care professionals a realistic view of the challenges, blessings, and personal discoveries experienced while caring for a loved one with Alzheimer's disease. Bob's recommendations for navigating the health care system to obtain a correct diagnosis, enduring emergency room visits and hospital admissions, advocating during long term care, and embracing hospice will be of benefit to every person caring for a loved one with dementia.

Deborah H. Perkins M.S., A.P.R.N., GNP-BC, GCNS-BC
Geriatric Nurse Practitioner and Clinical Nurse Specialist

Alzheimer's – The Identity Thief of the 21ˢᵗ Century is the most inspiring book that I have ever read. It shows the struggle that one caring for someone with a dementia disease and also the struggle for the person with the disease. Bob has shared many personal stories that would have meaning to any care partner. His lessons learned at the end of each chapter are inspiring. Through this book, Sarah continues to teach all of us about the long journey of a dementia disease, the struggles, the heartache but most importantly, the humor needed for the journey. In the stories, Bob gives the struggle but also the strength required to be a care partner. This book is different from most because of the sharing of the stories and the acknowledgement that everyone's experience is unique but has some common patterns. The book left me with hope that a person can survive being a care partner and also hope for the future when one day, we will have a cure.

Mary Ann Johnson, MA, Program Director, Alzheimer's Association Greater Richmond Chapter

Alzheimer's – The Identity Thief of the 21ˢᵗ Century is a true love story and an awesome tribute to Sarah's memory. Readers get a unique and realistic accounting of the trials and tribulations of everyday life after an average person is diagnosed with a dementing illness. It is inspirational and conveys hope through the present and future, in spite of the death sentence that has been dealt for this couple. As a career health care professional, I was speechless, honored, inspired and overwhelmed by the recognition and gratitude expressed for the time and effort of those involved in the often forgotten 'helping profession.' That was special to me since the Schaefer family was consumed by their long, tedious and often negative journey, yet they found the time to appreciate us and to say thank you. It is packed with hints and suggestions that should assist family as well as professional care givers to excel, while working in this important field. I am happy, grateful, and privileged to have been a part of this wonderful and memorable journey.

Kelly Mills Nixon, Hospice RN, Colonial Heights, VA.

Alzheimer's – The Identity Thief of the 21st Century provides a very personal description of the challenges and ultimate rewards of caring for a loved-one who suffers from dementia. In this case, the author, Bob Schaefer, provided the most intense and challenging care as the care partner for his wife, Sarah. Of particular benefit to others who are also on this care journey is the section that describes the various 'hats' that the care partner must wear. I would recommend this book to families as well as professionals in the aging network.

Bill Peterson, MSW, PhD, Richmond, Virginia

As an instructor of Alzheimer's disease and dementia for first responders for the Commonwealth of Virginia, and former employee of the Alzheimer's Association—Southeastern Virginia Chapter, I have had the honor of knowing and teaching audiences with Bob for well over a decade. I have watched Bob navigate the uncertainties of Alzheimer's disease ravaging his wife year after year and been witness to Bob's love, worries, frustrations, and ultimate loss of his beautiful wife, Sarah.

I am pleased that Bob chose to write this book as a tribute to his beloved wife knowing how proud she would feel that her story might make the journey of other caregivers a little easier to bear. Bob and Sarah's story is one of exceptional faith, love, hope, humor and understanding, and ultimately, healing.

This book is a candid depiction of Bob's experiences caring for Sarah over twenty-one years and his lessons learned from the onset of the disease, to the aftermath of her passing. Bob not only includes suggestions for dealing with various issues and crises that arise, but relates his own frustrations, reactions, and thoughts during each incident. Bob also shares with readers some of the darker depressing thoughts he experienced while caring for his wife that are seldom verbalized or discussed openly by caregivers.

Bob speaks openly about how this disease tested his own beliefs and spirituality in his 8th Chapter, *Where Was God?* He admitted that he "continued to go to church and pray on a regular basis to spite God," thinking he was fooling God by doing the exact opposite of what He would have expected him to do. Bob goes on to reveal how God was there all along, just not in ways that he could see nor understand at the time.

Anyone caring for their loved one in any capacity will learn many lessons from this book and its author who reinforces the idea to all of us that love, faith, patience, and understanding can weather any storm.

Julie Ana Skone, MS.Ed, Alzheimer's Training Coordinator, Commonwealth of Virginia, Department of Criminal Justice Services

ACKNOWLEDGEMENTS

I thank God for our forty-three year marriage. He loaned Sarah to me for the special time that we shared together. Also I thank Him for answering many of my prayers and the privilege of being at Sarah's bedside when she was taken to her heavenly reward. And finally thanks to God for permitting Sarah to educate me so that I could share that knowledge to help other victims of this disease and their care-partners.

I dedicate this book to Sarah's memory. God chose her to struggle for an extended period of time because she was special and so that others might benefit from her trials and tribulations. She made me the patient, caring, giving, sensitive, and loving man that I am today. I followed her example throughout our marriage. Without her wisdom, love, support and encouragement, I would not have been able to do the things that I did over the years.

I thank our children, their spouses and our eleven grandchildren. Without their unending love and support and their meetings of concern, wisdom, sensitivity and nurturing at the time of their mother's death, I would not be here writing this book. Had they not stepped forward and motivated me to regroup, I would have been lost. Thank you Thomas & Lori and children, Kelsey & Kyle; Sean & Robin and children, Corey, Taylor & Megan; Jennifer & Robert Jr. and children, Tristen,

Trey & Mikayla; Kathy & Scott and children, Kourtney, Sommer & Holly for your love and encouragement.

I thank my sister, Jackie for her prayers, frequent calls of support and visits to assist with Sarah's care. I appreciate her unending love which helped to maintain my sanity and focus.

Thank you to the couples that kept in touch with us during the years that Sarah struggled with her Alzheimer's. Those include Bill & Beverly Didie, Stoneybrook, New York; Don & Rosemary Harper, Myrtle Beach, South Carolina; Melinda & Bob Nobbs, Kew Gardens, New York. Thank you from the bottom of my heart for being there. Your regular calls, visits, unending love, prayers and support helped motivate me to keep my faith and dodge the curve balls that were thrown in my path.

Thank you to two special friends who have kept in touch and monitored my health and well-being. Theresa McDonald, who serves at the FBI Academy in Quantico, Virginia, and Barbara Zebro, my former secretary at the Norfolk, Virginia, Office of the FBI. They too regularly offered support, especially when the going got rough. Barbara, who was familiar with my writing style, was kind enough to proofread the first draft of my book.

Thank you to Julie Skone, Alzheimer's Training Coordinator, First Responder Training, Commonwealth of Virginia, Department of Criminal Justice Services for doing her part to keep me in touch with reality. Julie and I have trained First Responders for more than ten years. She made sure that I worked all over Virginia to divert my attention whenever the pressures of my role as a care-partner overwhelmed me. Julie was there whenever I wanted to talk. She proofread several chapters of this book and offered constructive criticism that assisted me to complete final drafts.

Thank you to MaryAnn Johnson, Program Director, Greater Richmond Chapter of the Alzheimer's Association. MaryAnn acted was a sounding board for me during my daily struggles through the world of Alzheimer's disease. She encouraged me to stay active with volunteer work. She made sure that I did not sit idle, so that negativism could take control of my life. She supported and encouraged me to finish this book. She was a second editor, who offered valuable suggestions, which when implemented improved the quality of my work.

I thank my son Bobby, who edited what was to have been the final draft of my book. He suggested ways that it could be further developed and fine tuned. He took time away from his beautiful family during the Christmas season to accomplish this. I am proud and flattered that he contributed to this tribute to his mother.

Thank you to that special person who helped me so much immediately after Sarah's death, especially at Christmas time. The special tender loving care (TLC) offered at the lowest point in my life helped me to keep my wits about me, as I floundered aimlessly in the sea of sorrow. That also encouraged me to want to survive and grow rather than self-destruct. I am so grateful for the love, help and support. I will never ever forget what you did for me.

Finally, let me recognize those individuals and organizations that have permitted me to use their knowledge, information or data as follows:

a. John Burroughs Foundation, for use of John Burroughs' quotation – "Leap and the net will appear."

b. Richmond Times-Dispatch for use of their picture of 'Our Hands' on the front cover.

c. Julie Skone for her computer analogy.

d. WVEC TV Norfolk, Virginia for use of Gray Matters—Issues in Aging .

e. James Wagenvoord, for the 'Commandments of Masculinity' from his book titled, Men—A Book For Women, 1978.

f. CBS Operations Inc. owners of all rights to Mighty Mouse properties for use of 'Might Mouse' and the slogan, "Here I am to save the day."

g. Joenetta Hendel for her poem, I'll Always Remember You.

h. Edgar Albert Guest for his poem, Miss Me, But Let Me Go. Joenetta Hendel for her poem, Don't Tell Me That You Understand.

FOREWORD

It is with mixed emotions of awe, inspiration and dread that I write this forward to Bob Schaefer's work of love dedicated to the memory of his wife Sarah and the life they lived in their 21 year battle with Alzheimer's disease. A powerful and passionate tapestry of Bob and Sarah's life is told with genuine authenticity and with such clarity that I am now brought to tears just as I did when I first read the manuscript.

I am in awe of Bob's internal fortitude, heart, and soul in his efforts of caring for Sarah but also in his cathartic writing for the purpose of helping others in their care of loved ones with Alzheimer's and related dementias. Bob has also inspired me to encourage others, and hopefully through reading his book you will also be strengthened by his message of love. And, it is also with dread that I write the forward, after being the first healthcare provider to have diagnosed Sarah with Alzheimer's Disease at the age of 50 as well as to write something of substance and meaning in tribute to Bob's message. This book is both timely and of marked significance, as 77 million baby boomers have reached the threshold of maturity for Alzheimer's disease to become present in their lives.

As a Neuropsychologist, I have had firsthand knowledge of working with Alzheimer's disease and related dementias. However, my experience of diagnosing neurological disorders in an office pales in comparison to the reality of living through the daily grind of increasing memory loss, confusion and the erosion of Sarah's beautiful life affirming personality. Bob writes that his survival was "…only made possible by an unlimited supply of faith and love with truckloads of patience and humor…", and he maintains that humor is a gift from God helping man to survive. Bob's strong Christian faith and sense of humor helped him survive, where he wrote "…Sarah answered what she thought was the telephone. She picked up the television remote and shouted, 'Hello, hello, hello. Who is this?' She glanced over at me and saw that I was already talking on the phone. She looked at the remote as she put it on the coffee table and we both began laughing hysterically. It was another example of her using the comic defense that I had worked so hard to teach her earlier. It was great that it still worked at times". This was at a time when Sarah was confused when the phone rang, and she would become frustrated and cry as she could not find the phone even when it was in front of her.

The book also provides a practical message, as Bob is a can-do guy and problem solver, which stemmed from his early years as a State Trooper and then later as an FBI Agent. The book is written in the memory of Sarah, but its purpose is to be a guide to others providing familiar milestones in the uncertain journey in caring for a loved one who has Alzheimer's Disease or a related dementia. By making the unfamiliar familiar, uncertainty and fear are countered by knowledge and experience. In this manner Bob describes Alzheimer's disease as "The Identity Thief", which robs one of their individuality—a very chilling but accurate description. It is a slow erosion of one's essence, which Dr. Paul Aravich, nationally recognized neuroscientist, called the "Internal Terrorist Threat".

Bob unmasks the true description of Alzheimer's disease, and renames care-givers as Care-Partners whom God drafts as special people which give unique meaning to the experience. He wrote that this new perspective "…strengthened me to strive toward survival, rather than finding myself a second victim of the disease". This model of being a Care-Partner, drafted by God through faith and hope, outlines five developmental stages: Denial and Depression, Resentment and Anger, Alteration of Personality, Frenzy and Tolerance. These stages of development in a Care-Partner became a reality for Bob and he hopes that they will be a guide to others as milestones on their own journeys.

Through each chapter Bob guides the reader through the various stages of development of a Care-Partner with personal experiences. He offers strategies of approach in dealing with the inevitable changes and ends each chapter with lessons learned as the take home message. Sarah's last letter, as written by Bob, integrates the book in an intimate closure of love, respect and dignity. May Bob's words be an inspiration to all of the unsung Care-Partner heroes caring for those with Alzheimer's disease and a related dementia?

Scott W. Sautter, Ph.D., FACPN, Virginia Beach, Virginia

Table of Contents

INTRODUCTION

Coping with Alzheimer's disease is challenging and mind boggling to say the least. It is difficult to believe that so little is known about it. If the top researchers and doctors across the country are not convinced what causes it, then how will a treatment or cure be found?

5.5 million Americans have already been diagnosed. The latest statistics from the Alzheimer's Association indicate that someone is diagnosed every seventy seconds. Without a treatment or a cure in the near future, it is anticipated that 10—million baby boomers will become victims of this disease. At that time, a human will be diagnosed every 30 rather than 70 seconds.

I use care-partner rather than caretaker or caregiver because that best describes the role that you fill. Success means partnering with your loved one who has been diagnosed, as well as with family & friends, physician, elder attorney, emergency room personnel, hospitals, pharmacies, and the local chapter of the Alzheimer's Association, to mention just a few.

My job was spine chilling and the most strenuous, long-drawn-out battle that I ever fought in my life. It is a death sentence for its victims and far too often for those drafted as care-partners. It profoundly affects everyone in a family or circle of friends, but especially those functioning as full-time care-partners.

We receive an abundance of education in our fast paced society; however, we are not instructed about the specifics of death. That is a forbidden topic, which tends to put us at a disadvantage in our role as a care-partner for a demented person.

Hope and support are available for care-partners who are willing to be proactive and take chances. Never let your guard down on this journey and lose those abilities. There is always hope, which will be paramount to your survival. Researchers work day and night and will soon solve the mystery of Alzheimer's. A treatment, if not a cure, is on the horizon. Do not fail to keep that in sight.

I chose Alzheimer's – the Identity Thief of the 21st Century as my title for a special reason. From the beginning, I want those powerful words to be on the mind of every care-partner. They are filled with conviction and hope, while at the same time stressing that you are in charge of your own destiny, if you are willing to take chances. They encourage care-partners to be proactive and to neutralize this horrendous disease with faith, hope, humor, love, patience and understanding. Do not wait for something to happen or solve itself. Be on the lookout for new and innovative ideas to deal with problems and the challenging behaviors that you will encounter. Think and react on your feet. Do not restrict yourself to thinking the same old thoughts and solutions. If you always do what you've always done, you'll always be what you've always been. Hide not your talents, for what is a sundial in the shade? Faith will guide you through the tough times and the safety net will always be there if you should fail. Think outside the box. Make that your primary weapon of choice in the fight against Alzheimer's disease.

My first thought after Sarah's diagnosis was that God drafts special people to be Alzheimer's/dementia care-partners. Those words were reassuring and gave my care-partner role unique meaning. I was strengthened and encouraged to strive toward survival, rather than being a second victim of the disease. They gained more and more credibility every day that I had the opportunity and privilege of being a care-partner for Sarah during her journey.

The intense and never ending stress of a care-partner can often lead to negativism. I thought outside the box and selected the word draft to set a positive tone. I identified developmental steps that care-partners will likely experience, while caring for their loved ones with dementia. These are not based on data collected during a formal or scientific study. Rather, they are my observations and experiences from my 35—years in the law enforcement community, as well as 21—years as a full-time care-partner and care-manager for Sarah.

Hopefully, becoming familiar with and understanding these milestones and how they affected Sarah's and my life will better prepare new and seasoned care-partners for their careers. They should provide a positive tool to better educate and help care-partners for their difficult and ongoing challenge. These milestones should help one to avoid many of the pitfalls that I faced and was beaten by during my journey into the unknown.

Our story will also help demonstrate how these unique stages unfold for the average, everyday care-partner. Everyone with Alzheimer's/dementia is unique in their progression of this destructive disease but they all tend to follow some flexible and loose fitting patterns. MaryAnn Johnson, Program Director, Greater Richmond Chapter of the Alzheimer's Association says, "If you have seen one person with Alzheimer's disease, you have seen one person with Alzheimer's disease." All victims of this disease are individuals, which makes each and every one of them travel a unique path during their progression.

There are patterns, similarities and guidelines, but behavior will normally vary from individual to individual.

Care-partners will not adhere strictly to every aspect of my model of stages. They will progress at their own pace. Some may become stuck in one or more of the milestones for a period of time or perhaps for the duration of their journey, which could result in their loved ones outliving them. It should become obvious that those individuals are having difficulty accepting and adapting to their challenging role as a care-partner. Attitude and perception adjustments must be made continually during a care-partner's journey through faith and hope, in order to become a survivor rather than becoming a second victim.

My model sets forth five steps of development that should become a reality for a care-partner during the progression of a dementing illness. I call my model 'draft' as a reminder that care-partners are mostly drafted rather than volunteering for this unbelievably difficult role in our society. Each stage will be described in a separate chapter of this book.

Milestone #1 – Denial & Depression
Milestone #2 – Resentment & Anger
Milestone #3 – Alteration of Personality
Milestone #4 – Frenzy
Milestone #5—Tolerance

Chapter 1
TO REACH MY DESTINATION

We lived in Virginia Beach, Virginia. Sarah worked as a medical assistant for a surgeon, while I served as a Supervisory Special Agent in the Norfolk Office of the FBI. We were extremely happy until Alzheimer's Disease unexpectedly came along and took over our lives. This is the story of how our lives, feelings and emotions changed for the good and the bad.
(Bob – 1/15/10)

Alzheimer's disease is a degenerative, progressive brain disorder that affects memory, thought, behavior, personality, and muscle control of human beings. It is a physical disease that attacks and kills brain cells, as it steals a person's identity.

This is Sarah's and my story presented in a way to give you hope and belief in the future in spite of your exposure to this predicament that has created such havoc in your life. I call Alzheimer's disease 'The Identity Thief of the 21st Century;' consequently, I will lean toward the world of technology in which we live. I direct your attention to Julie Skone, Alzheimer's Training Coordinator, Department of Criminal Justice Services, Commonwealth of Virginia, who profoundly came up with an analogy that she presented at an Alzheimer's – First Responder Training Seminar. Ms. Skone uniquely compared a diagnosis of Alzheimer's to a virus on your computer. Her words mirrored my thoughts and I felt compelled to present them to parlay my own emotions.

Ms. Skone said, "A simple way to think about Alzheimer's disease and how it affects the brain is to compare it to a computer virus. It should be noted that there is no current research to indicate that Alzheimer's disease is caused by any type of a virus. This is simply an analogy that I made up to keep pace with the 21st Century and the age of technology. My goal is to better describe and to simply show how Alzheimer's wipes out memory and cripples the functioning of the human brain.

Please think of your brain as if it was your own personal computer. As such, it would be responsible for all for all the workings of your brain, as well as the housing all of your memories. Our brains would have a soft-drive just like our computers that store temporary or short term memories. At the same time, our permanent or deep rooted memories and significant events would be stored in our hard-drive. Our personal computer or brain has millions and millions of memory files, some that are shared or common information and some that are completely unique to each and every individual. Everything that we have learned, experienced, or encountered has a memory file and is stored somewhere in our computer or brain.

Our temporary memories stored on our soft-drive are things that we learn very quickly and that fade or are completely forgotten within a short period of time, i.e. names, daily to-do lists, and the like. These are events and information not significant enough to transfer into our long-term data bank or hard-drive.

Our long-term memory bank or hard-drive stores important information such as skills and abilities, significant people in our lives, and events from a long time ago. Everything that we learned how to do since the day that we were born is stored on our hard-drive. Some of these memories are stored in files that are not accessed or opened often, but they can be retrieved easily if something triggers those memories. For instance, when a person that you haven't thought about in a long, long time appears on your Facebook page, or you see them in a picture, their name will trigger that memory file to open.

As we age, we accumulate more and more memory files and sometimes it will take a little longer to access information that we are seeking because we now have so, so many files to access; however, in time, we will be able to locate and open the correct file.

Alzheimer's disease acts like a computer virus and damages the memory files in your brain. It begins by wreaking havoc on the soft-drive, or the temporary, short-term information first. It often short-circuits and redirects information to the wrong files. For example, if you have an uncle named Bob, the virus could redirect your "Bob" file, and open the wrong one, leading you to believe that Bob is your brother and not your uncle. You will naturally insist that this information is correct, because your brain has told you that it is true and your brain does not normally lie to you. At this point, it will be near impossible to convince an individual suffering from Alzheimer's disease that what they are saying is not true or real. Their brain has told them that it is true and how can you argue with your brain?

This computer virus in the form of Alzheimer's disease will begin deleting files in the soft-drive and eventually in the hard-drive or long-term memory too, making it impossible to remember how to perform the simplest of tasks, such as cooking, dressing, bathing, or eating, or who your uncle Bob is at all. A person's brain will lose the ability to remember people, objects, and information simply because the memory files in their personal computer have been deleted.

Actual computer viruses are insidious and invisible unless you are a computer whiz, but there are normally signs that something has gone wrong with the computer. Fatal error messages may begin popping up and the computer will shut down by itself. When this happens, I usually go into the denial mode thinking that the computer will somehow fix itself because the idea that my computer will eventually crash is way too difficult for me to understand and accept.

Alzheimer's disease acts in a similar manner. Initially, signs appear – lapses in memory, losing or misplacing things, changes in personality and behavior, but these signs are subtle and easy to dismiss or deny. Family members often attempt to rationalize that such deficits are often due to age, depression, stress, and medications. Eventually the symptoms become so pronounced that a doctor's visit is in order and a diagnosis of dementia results."

With the above in mind, understand that Alzheimer's disease swallows the brain of a human being, but is not always able to take total control of the feelings, emotions and the heart of its victim. I have observed individuals who often continue to have the capacity to love, experience feelings and emotions, although it may be limited. They also remember more than you might expect, even if they are not always in the present, or able to communicate on our terms.

Most care-partners are drafted without regard to race, color, creed, national origin, occupation or financial status. They are remarkable, warm, sensitive, sympathetic, helpful, loving, energetic, practical, and dependable beings. They assume a role in our society that most people would avoid at all costs. They are programmed to think only about their loved ones to the point that they neglect their own health and well-being. They perform unbelievable miracles as a trainer, coach, and cheerleader. They routinely think for two people, which is mind-boggling. It is no wonder that care-partners burnout or self-destruct.

Care-partners get up every morning to perform in an unbelievably stressful job. Not to take anything away from first responders or war heroes, but care-partners are true, unacknowledged heroes in our society. They perform in their own backyards and communities without receiving or expecting to receive pay, praise, or in most instances, even a thank you.

Police officers, firefighters, air traffic controllers, and high bridge steel workers are considered high stress occupations. I have never seen care-partners listed among the top ten most stressful roles in our society. I was an air traffic controller in the U.S. Navy and a law enforcement officer for thirty-five years. I can unequivocally say that the stress experienced in those so-called high stress occupations did not come close to matching the stress that I experienced as a full-time care-partner for my wife. This could be attributed to the uncertainty of the progression, the lack of knowledge or past training about the disease, and the fact that there is often no end in sight.

I was honored and privileged to have been drafted as my wife Sarah's care-partner. I was on the front lines working with, helping and protecting the most important person in the world to me at her time of need. I thank God that He chose me for that awesome responsibility. I learned something from Sarah every day in spite of the fact that Alzheimer's was narrowing her abilities. Although it was a tumultuous journey, I would not have wanted or expected it to be any other way. God tested us with 21 years of Alzheimer's disease.

Most victims will eventually enter into their own world, which can make them oblivious to the people around them. The behavior of a person with Alzheimer's may be irritating, unexplainable, and inconsistent, at best. The important point to understand is that the victims of this disease often retain many of their feelings and emotions, although in varying degrees. Those feelings and emotions are likely to appear when and where you least expect them to and in a variety of ways. This is when a skilled and dedicated care-partner will learn to understand and interpret body language as the key to continued communication.

There is no cure for Alzheimer's/dementia. In an absolute sense, no medication slows or stops the progression; consequently, a diagnosis is equivalent to a death sentence. Words cannot adequately describe what goes through the mind of a human being as this grim form of the identity thief robs them of everything that they know, as well as their very being and identity. Alzheimer's, which is age related, will undoubtedly become the identity thief of the 21st century. The seventy-seven million baby boomers coming of age should guarantee that.

The process of grieving, which is different for every individual, begins at the moment of diagnosis. It usually affects care-partners harder than those diagnosed with the disease. The grieving persists, while bits and pieces of your loved one's brain are pilfered. It is up to the care-partner to fight, grow and survive during this journey. Never give up hope that a cure and/or treatment will be discovered tomorrow. That is something that I prayed for and believed in until Sarah's death. I still pray daily and will continue that until a treatment or cure is found. I will never give up that hope.

The enormity a care-partner's job taking care of a family member or friend diagnosed with Alzheimer's disease or dementia cannot be easily described to someone who has never walked the walk; therefore, before looking at the milestones that care-partners will likely experience, I will set the stage mentally, so that you can appreciate the role of the full-time care-partner. I am living proof that with an abundance of faith, love, prayer, patience and perseverance, you can and will survive just as I have done. Hopefully, our story will help to make your journey easier? Knowing what to do and expect should assist you to safely negotiate the bumps in the road that will disrupt you on your journey. Never forget that I am just an ordinary and average Joe from New York City. If I survived, you can too.

I find it helpful to compare the full-time care-partner to a chameleon. Initially, that might seem like a strange comparison, but bear with me for a few minutes. A chameleon is one of the world's smallest reptiles. When it senses danger, it has the unique ability to change the color of its skin as a form of camouflage in order to protect itself and survive in its environment. A care-partner tends to do what a chameleon does; however, instead of changing the color of their skin for camouflage, care-partners change hats. Over time, as responsibilities become overwhelming, the changing of hats can involve an inordinate amount of time and energy. As a result, care-partners wear out quickly. Hopefully, they will quickly appreciate that changing hats is one of the best resources available to them on their voyage. The constant changing of hats, although it might seem burdensome and cumbersome will be worthwhile and lead to survival. Look at these 21 hats and see how you are and can be affected by their use.

Care-Partner Hats

1. Individual—Our background, upbringing and socialization make us different and unique.
2. Family Member—We are born into a family, which can be good or bad.
3. Spiritual Being—We usually reach out spiritually when the going gets rough rather than on a daily basis.
4. Alzheimer's Student—The more we educate yourself about Alzheimer's the better we will be able to cope with its progression.
5. Manager/ Leader—This can be dreaded by many.
6. Worker Bee—We do it all not only for ourselves, but also for our loved ones.
7. Enforcer—It is so difficult to be the bad guy.

8. Chief Cook, Bottle Washer & Pot Walloper—Where are my helpers? I cannot possibly do it all, especially while I am taking care of my loved day and night.

9. Maid—Some of us clean the house, do laundry, and dishes, but still cannot fold a fitted sheet.

10. Accountant—Math may be easy for some, but it is drudgery for others.

11. Chauffeur—Driving can be fun, but not when you are the only driver.

12. Actor/Actress—Entertainer – What have I gotten myself into here?

13. Activities Director—This could be a big mistake.

14. Nurse—This is insane with my limited training and experience.

15. Mommy—This may be okay for the women, but what about the men?

16. Communicator—This can be a stumbling block for many.

17. Social Worker—Some sensitivity required for this hat.

18. Alzheimer's Detective—No badge, gun or law enforcement experience needed to wear this hat.

19. Computer Geek—This can be more complicated for seniors.

20. Juggler—This comes into play with years of experience.

21. Fisherman or Hostage Negotiator—It is your choice.

I was shocked to find out that there were so many hats involved as a care-partner. Your journey can be easier when these hats are under your control. Ordinary citizens wear some of these hats at times; however, they are not forced to wear them all, 24/7, as care-partners often have to do. Realistically, care-partners never get any appreciable break from them. Familiarize yourself with them and use them to your advantage. Your job can be challenging, difficult and even dangerous; however, when these hats at your disposal you will adapt to situations that you will face.

As an FBI agent, I worked with the victims of shooting incidents. I learned that they responded automatically when they were called upon to fire their weapons in life threatening situations. That automatic reaction was the result of the hours of training that agents received on the range. Education will help to ensure an automatic and proper response to the needs of your loved one. It will also encourage you to think outside the box at the same time. I cannot overemphasize the importance of education to make your job easier and more rewarding.

Individual is the first hat that a care-partner is called upon to wear. Whether male or female, we are all individuals. Our background and rearing makes each of us unique. We develop personalities during the socialization process that kicks in after our birth. We are educated at differing levels as we mature. Our maturity level and personality will factor into our acceptance of and performance as a care-partner. Many of us will marry and have families of our own. We should work in our chosen careers until we are touched by Alzheimer's disease.

I earned a Master's in Public Administration (MPA) and worked in the Criminal Justice field for thirty-five years. I was seven years from retirement at the time that Sarah began exhibiting signs of dementia. I do not believe that educational level or chosen profession has much to do with your role as a care-partner with the exception of those who work in and are educated as health care professionals. In some instances, that could be a hindrance rather than an asset. It doesn't matter if you are a male or a female when you are drafted to be a care-partner. I have seen both perform well and poorly. There is no formula to determine who will perform well. It is not unusual for many individuals to be at or near retirement, when this crisis strikes.

Family Member is another hat that care-partners will be called upon to wear. We are born into families, which can be good or bad. Family members and siblings rally around and assist each other, as they move through the normal socialization process. Family size does not normally make a difference when traumatic incidents like Alzheimer's strike. Distance away from the family member diagnosed with Alzheimer's can easily influence the life of a care-partner. We have responsibilities as members of our immediate families. These can be in conflict with our role as a care-partner. The precise impact that Alzheimer's has depends upon which member of your family has been diagnosed. The reaction to the diagnosis of a parent will have most impact upon the spouse of that parent and their children. The reaction to the diagnosis of a grandparent will have more impact upon your parents then you. The impact of the diagnosis of a sibling will have more impact on the immediate family of that brother or sister then it will have for you as a brother or a sister. The relationship of the family member diagnosed will have the most influence upon and determine how a care-partner copes with their new role. Suffice it to say, that family dynamics present a challenge for all care-partners.

Spiritual Being is another hat to be considered. We reach out spiritually when the going gets rough rather than on a daily basis when our lives are stable. That is human nature. In most instances, a care-partner as a spiritual being gains the necessary strength from his/her religious beliefs that are in place at the time that a crisis occurs. The results will vary again because we are all individuals. Alzheimer's is a devastating diagnosis, which can elicit a negative reaction from you as a spiritual being.

I had strong religious beliefs, yet when this crisis occurred, I became angry with everyone and everything, including God. This intense period of anger is not unusual and should not be considered unhealthy. I was so angry at God that I decided to spite him by continuing to go to church, as if nothing had happened because He would expect me to reject Him and boycott religious services. I wanted desperately to outsmart God. That anger didn't last long. I will elaborate later how my faith helped me to become a survivor rather than a second victim of Alzheimer's disease.

Alzheimer's Student is the next hat that care-partners will likely wear. Most care-partners will research and study Alzheimer's and dementia. There is no other choice if you want to attempt to put yourself in a position to defeat it. This may be difficult for those who have been out of school for a long time. An insatiable thirst for knowledge grows as you tend to develop a fantasy that you will discover something that will help or make your loved one better. The focus of research centers on finding a miracle or proving that the doctors are wrong. These thoughts, as unrealistic as they might appear to be, will always be in the back of your mind, even as the disease has progressed into the final stage. This hat becomes an obsession for many. Research does help to fill those long, lonely, and sleepless nights. In reality, the more educated you become the better you should be able to cope with the progression.

Manager/Leader is another hat that must be worn. It is often perceived as a necessary evil. Part of the reluctance might be because of a lack of experience or possibly a desire to function in this capacity. Unfortunately, there is no one else available to assume that role and make things happen. You are compelled to think for two people – you and a spouse or parent or grandparent. You will exhaust yourself thinking continuously for two people. Initially, it might not be a problem because of the novelty of the situation; however, in time, it will take its toll on the average care-partner.

All of my time and effort was directed toward my career as a Supervisory Special Agent in the FBI. I was not accustomed to managing the household too because Sarah had always done that. There simply wasn't enough time and effort left over at the end of my workday for that. I had to reorganize and reprioritize to make this hat work.

The Worker Bee hat can dominate your life once it appears. You think that you are already doing it all and all of a sudden more gets dumped on you. You are not only the boss, but also the gofer to carry out all of the necessary tasks and responsibilities, not only for your loved one, but also for yourself. Sadly, you are the only one that can make this happen. It is more difficult than it sounds.

We live in a fast paced society. There is barely enough time to get everything done that is expected of us, especially if you work. All of a sudden, you are doing everything for two. The theme becomes work – work – work. Remember, thus far, I have only identified half of the care-partner hats that you will be expected to wear. The potential for adding hats is never ending. It leads to burnout, poor health or mental problems.

Enforcer hat is not always a favorite among care-partners. Decisions must be made and problems need to be solved in a timely fashion for the sake of your loved one. It often requires you to be the bad guy in sensitive and important areas such as—Can my spouse still be left alone? Can your grandparent cook safely? Should your spouse or parent be driving? Is it time for a long-term care facility?

It doesn't matter, if the decision is about medications, finances, or behaviors, care-partners must be the enforcer. This will not always make you the most popular person with your loved one. Decisions might not always be in concert with the thoughts of other family members. You will use this hat daily. It may raise your stress, self-control and patience levels.

The Chief Cook, Bottle Washer & Pot Walloper hat can be good or a hassle depending upon your background. Where is the maid? I do not know how nor do I want to do this alone with everything else that I already have to do. The chief cook part was okay. However, the bottle washer piece was stressful. This may be the case for many care-partners, especially males who are not accustomed to such responsibilities. It is one thing to have to prepare the meals, but definitely a downside having to clean up, especially with everything else that you are doing.

I love to cook especially on gas or a charcoal grill. It has been a hobby and stress reducer. I was challenged creating food dishes for our family, friends, especially on special occasions. This may not be the case for all care-partners, especially if cooking is not in your background or one of your preferences. Eventually, the chief cook hat didn't fit me any longer. I'm sure that it is or will be the same for many care-partners when it becomes more of a nuisance rather than a challenge or fun.

Sarah's eating habits and abilities fluctuated drastically as the identity thief progressed. I tried to find foods and meals that appealed to her changing and often erratic taste buds, but she lost weight in spite of my effort and hard work. My research, resourcefulness and innovativeness were in vain. My role as chief cook became stressful when I realized that I could no longer prepare and feed Sarah the balanced diet that I thought she needed. I can imagine how stressful it can become for a care-partner who has never had any experience preparing foods. This is when TV dinners or prepared meals from the local market are likely to be used; however, that can become an expensive venture. Adaptation and innovativeness will lead toward survival. Do whatever you need to do to keep your loved one happy and healthy.

The Maid is one that I never dreamed wearing myself. It is another responsibility that can go either way. I am not belittling the profession; I guess it is a guy thing. It was difficult for me to wear. I perceive myself to be the macho veteran of 35 years in law enforcement that does not do housework. I learned to clean the house, do the laundry and dishes, but still cannot fold a fitted sheet. I overcame that fantasy by making a conscious effort to adapt to, wear and accept the maid hat as another challenge that comes as part of the care-partner package. I hate to admit it, but I have always shared some of the cleaning responsibilities with Sarah during our marriage. That made it easier to wear this hat. I thought that it only involved a limited amount of light cleaning, which I could handle. I discovered that there was much more involved. I forgot about the washer and dryer, the dishwasher, folding and ironing laundry, washing windows, dusting, cleaning bathrooms, and shampooing carpets. For some, cleaning becomes unnecessary and almost a nuisance. It forces a care-partner to prioritize, which tends to put the maid hat toward the bottom of the list. Keeping your loved one occupied, happy, safe, preventing them from wandering away and getting lost becomes so much more important than cleaning.

One of the worst parts of the maid hat surfaced when Sarah resented me doing the cleaning she had done in the past. She lost the ability to perform most activities, including cleaning. She recognized and was troubled by those losses. That was difficult to watch. Fortunately, as with many activities that are taken away by dementia, they soon completely forget about them. That is a good thing for the victim, although it does not make it easier for the care-partner. Sarah was quick to forget, but I and most care-partners remembered and grieved those losses.

The Accountant hat is not a favorite for some care-partners. Math may be easy for some, but it is drudgery for others. I feared wearing it even though I had been a math and an accounting major in college, at least for a short period of time. I learned to hate and detest anything that involved numbers. I gladly relinquished that responsibility to Sarah during the early days of our marriage. Sarah had a knack for juggling figures to prevent us from suffering financially, especially during our difficult and lean years. It was a shock for me to take over that responsibility. I hated it, but had to get over it quickly when I realized that I had no other choice but to face the demon and make the best of it. The omen fell on me as a care-partner. It is no surprise that care-partners flounder and are overwhelmed by the hats that they are saddled with. The key is to adapt to the wearing of these hats as soon as is possible. The longer that you resist these responsibilities, even if you detest or feel uncomfortable with them, the tougher the journey will be for you. Understanding that life is a series of adaptations should help care-partners to set a positive tone for their lives.

Chauffeur is an easy hat to wear. It was for me because I have always loved to drive. It must be related to my career in law enforcement, especially my earlier years on the road as a trooper. Sarah loved to ride in the car, but only as a passenger. It was therapy for her, especially after her diagnosis. I had to make sure that I had a pillow and a blanket to keep comfortable and warm and a place for her to put her feet on the dashboard. Grocery shopping, the hospital, doctor and dental visits, picking up prescriptions, vacations, banking, dining, visiting family and friends, all require time in the car. Once again, like it or not, you as a care-partner must do all of the driving. My chauffeur's hat came in handy when Sarah went through the phase of wanting to go home. The chauffeur's hat might not seem like much initially, but it will become burdensome in time.

The Actor/Actress hat is an important and tedious part of your care-partner responsibilities. This will likely become more and more burdensome as the identity thief progresses into and beyond the middle stage. It will sneak up when you least expect it and are overwhelmed and stressed beyond your tolerance limits. When your loved one is less able to do things, there will be a tendency for the both of you to get depressed. This can affect behaviors.

Sarah, as is common for many victims of dementia, felt losses as she experienced them, although she might not have always been able to verbalize them. As abilities and activities decrease, they will likely be replaced with verbal complaints, repetition, depression, sleeping, pacing, and wandering. All will have a tendency to aggravate care-partners. Unfortunately, you will not have the luxury of feeling sick or out of sorts, or being in a bad mood, or wanting to be left alone. You will be forced to put on an act to make your loved one believe that you are happy and content. This is true when your loved one uses you as a sounding board or displays other annoying behaviors. It is difficult to ignore the consequences of Alzheimer's, and put a smile on your face or forget the insults that you have heard. This can become emotionally exhausting, especially when you are so upset about the demon that you are facing.

The Activity Director's hat will become important as your loved one becomes more dependent upon you for all of their wants and needs. You will be preoccupied with making sure that your loved one is occupied, mentally challenged, happy and positive. Sarah was able to do things for herself in the early stage. She thought, reasoned, and planned without much effort. She worked, drove, babysat for her grandchildren, shopped, cooked, cleaned, socialized, went boating, traveled, used the telephone, watched television, read books and newspapers, played bridge, and worked on crypto quotes and puzzles. She occupied herself without assistance. She was happy with herself and not depressed. However, as the middle stage approached, the activity director's hat came to the forefront.

It was a sad when Sarah had to rely upon me as her care-partner for everything. As meaningful activities slowly slipped away, boredom, which is a negative stressor, became more apparent. The easiest of activities became a burden and a source of embarrassment. These losses were replaced with less desirable and annoying behaviors. Watching soap operas, walking and caring for our dog Skipper were the last of her interests to vanish. These were replaced by a nonstop need to wander and pick at her face and forehead, until it bled. I had to step up to the plate and work overtime to keep boredom at a minimal level. That was not the easiest of feats and at times it was near impossible.

Sarah was obsessed with helping me do the household chores, but she was no longer able to follow instructions or doing anything on her own. I was losing control by wearing so many hats at the same that Sarah was losing control of her very being. Dementia was beating me. I relied on my available repertoire of activities that had always interested her. I used them daily, but tried to rotate them as often as was possible. I tried my best to keep Sarah on a regular schedule. Often, it will be the simple things that are life savers. Do not overlook support groups as a valuable source of information concerning everything from activities to personal care.

The activities director hat requires constantly searching for new and innovative ways to prevent your loved one from getting bored. This will become a major issue. The internet and the Alzheimer's Association are available to support you when it the activity director's hat becomes burdensome. Reaching out and partnering should be part of every care-partners arsenal of weapons that help to prevent burnout. Avoid becoming lazy, which will tend to trick you into reinventing the wheel, which is a waste of time and effort. I suggest a web based resources program called the Edge Project. This valuable resource is provided by the New York State Department of Health, Office of Continuing Care.

The Nurse hat is likely to come and go sporadically throughout your entire career as a care-partner. Unless there are other medical problems, it should not be frequently worn during the earlier stages. Usage increases as your loved one's immune system and health are weakened, destroyed and compromised. This hat can be the most frightening of all of the hats that you will have to wear. My training and experience amounted to first aid courses during my law enforcement years. I started off as a nursing student, but years of experience gradually moved me to the position of a registered nurse handling everything from medications to enemas. It amazed me how quickly I learned to adapt to a new situation, especially when there was no other choice.

My biggest fear throughout the progression was that I would not recognize and admit when I was performing beyond my capabilities. This hat became increasingly more difficult as the activities of daily living withered away and disappeared. I was pleased at my performance as Sarah's nurse during the fifteen years that she was at home with me. In the latter stage, I took Sarah's vitals and recorded any and all changes in her life that appeared pertinent to her progression.

The Mommy hat does not appear naturally for every care-partner, especially males who are not accustomed to wearing it. It is okay for the women, but often a chore for the men. It is usually worn from day one. You, as a care-partner, perform all that is necessary to keep your loved one happy, safe, comfortable, and content just as any mother does for her child or children. It becomes a natural instinct for you as a care-partner. I am not saying that persons with dementing illnesses engage in childlike behavior. This is a pet peeve of mine. They are adults, who through no fault of their own, are no longer able to perform at a level that is appropriate for their age and at the same time acceptable by society. They are full of knowledge and life's experiences, but have difficulty retrieving and communicating those experiences, feelings and emotions to others.

The Communicator hat is another of the most important, but often overlooked or ignored care—partner resources. Reaching out and communicating with other family members, friends, neighbors, clergy, doctors, attorneys, pharmacists, or anyone that you interface with is often a key to success. Care-partners must learn quickly to communicate well and effectively on the good and the bad days. This is not always the strongest instruments for spouses and family members. Communication can be a major obstacle during the middle and latter stages of the progression. It also can be a challenge to hold one's own with other family members who have not had an opportunity to walk in your shoes. There is no way that they can or will understand the stress that a care-partner experiences on a daily basis. This hat should theoretically help families and friends to work together toward a pleasant environment.

Social Worker is another hat worn frequently by a care-partner. It often presents another challenge by requiring more sensitivity and understanding than might be available. A care-partner will strive to enhance the quality of life and develop the full potential of their loved one. He will make every effort to comfort them throughout their terminal illness. This will require that you communicate and negotiate with family members, individuals and groups of all types and sizes. Your long-term goal will be overcoming the stumbling blocks that will be in your path. It will consume an inordinate amount of time, effort, and innovativeness, which might be in short supply as your loved one reaches the final stage. You will become extremely frustrated when you work with the bureaucracies that regulate assisted living and long-term care facilities, social security, Medicare, Medicaid, veterans' benefits, and the like. A care-partner wears the social worker hat 24/7 and not just for a forty hour week.

The Alzheimer's Detective hat might seem unusual or bizarre to anyone who does not have experience working in law enforcement. None is needed for this hat. When you think about it, it makes perfect sense. I spent decades as a criminal investigator struggling to find answers to the age old questions of who, what, where, when, why, and how. These answers are critical to solving crimes. They will definitely assist in the handling of unusual behaviors that arise in the later stages of dementia. The life of a full-time care-partner will require the daily use of detective skills to avoid catastrophic reactions. You will not be a sworn officer nor carry a badge and a gun. You won't write out tickets or make arrests, but you will be charged with keeping the peace and assuring that your loved one is safe and secure. You will put into service the same skills that a successful investigator uses to solve crimes. You might never have ever thought of it that way, but you will actually be an Alzheimer's detective.

The Computer Geek hat emerges naturally for care-partners who are computer literate. The computer provides comfort and may even evolve into one of your best companions. This can cause anger and frustration for those who are intimidated by or who have not mastered the internet. It is the world's largest library for resource assistance as well as a post office. The computer can have a positive impact if it opens new doors. An example might be communicating by e-mail with other care-partners who are experiencing similar difficulties, which can be an informal way to debrief themselves and others in the comfort of their homes. The important point is that they never have to leave their loved one's side to accomplish this. It extends the boundaries of formal support groups, especially during a crisis situation. This is when modern technology supports care-partners and can make their lives more bearable.

The Juggler hat is worn after years of practical and hands-on experience as a full-time and front-line care-partner. It requires a combination of talent and experience. It develops into a second sense over time which permits them to excel in that role. Juggler empowers care-partners to wear the appropriate hat at the proper time. This intuition facilitates the managing of daily and unexpected stressors that are inherent in your role. Becoming proficient at the wearing this hat is critical to care-partner survival.

Fisherman and Hostage Negotiator are the last hats that care-partners are likely to wear. These two also tend to emerge after years of experience. You choose the one that you feel most comfortable wearing. Both can accomplish the same goal. The fisherman and the hostage negotiator normally think outside the box. This contributes to their success.

The fisherman drops one or more lines into the water with a favorite lure on the end of each. If he does not catch something within a reasonable amount of time, he changes the lure and tries again with a new one attached. He repeats that same pattern over and over again until he catches a fish. The same principle applies to a care-partner. Let's say that you want your loved one to do something. Perhaps it is getting them to the dinner table and they refuse. Back off and wait a few moments before asking them again. Divert their attention and try again. It is equivalent to the fisherman putting on a new lure on his line. Sweet talk your loved one or entice them with a certain food, dessert or sweet. It often requires more than one try or lure. If another family member is available have them ask your loved one to go to the table. It is important not to force or argue with them especially if they resist and become anxious. Keep in mind that changing the lure can help to keep peace and tranquility in the home. You must be prepared and get into the habit of continually change lures.

This same principle applies to the hostage negotiator, if you chose that over the fisherman. A hostage negotiator arrives at the scene of a crisis with the intention of manipulating the behavior of an individual. He always carries a bag of tricks with him. If one idea or trick does not work, he reaches into his bag and finds another that he can use. Sooner or later, with a little patience, skill, and luck, a negotiator usually succeeds. The same can be true for care-partners. Learn to think outside the box when your situation dictates that it is appropriate. Keep extra lures and a bag of tricks handy so that you can overcome whatever obstacles are placed in your path. Understand interests and desires and keep this repertoire handy to provide calm, reassuring distraction thereby using memory loss to your advantage. Learn to conduct a therapeutic manipulation.

Varied and often complex sources of anxiety will normally require that you wear and change the above hats. Sarah exhibited a tremendous amount of anxiety throughout the middle and late stage of her dementia. I, as a problem solver and investigator, prepared a list of all the sources of anxiety that I was able to identify. I then looked at whether or not I had any control over that source. If I did not, then it was necessary to determine which hat or hats I would wear to best cope with its effects. I changed hats like the chameleon changed colors in order to camouflage myself in the face of the increasing frustration, pain and discomfort. This was the only way to assure that I would continue to properly care for Sarah, while maintaining some semblance of sanity. Hopefully, reviewing these will help you to understand and appreciate how and why care-partners progress through the stages of development that I set forth in the next several chapters.

MEDICAL IN NATURE

- The disease itself
- Medications
- Hallucinations
- Illness – cold, flu, pneumonia, urinary tract infection, weakness and fatigue
- Pain (illness or injury)
- Allergy – rash
- Doctor or emergency room visit, surgery, hospital stay
- Constipation
- Poor eyesight, depth perception, loss of hearing (leading to misperceptions), loss of smell and/or taste
depression

ACTIVITIES OF DAILY LIVING

- brushing teeth
- bathing, showering, shampooing hair
- selecting clothing
- dressing, undressing, incontinence protection, soiled clothing
- ill-fitting clothing
- inability to use zippers or buttons
- getting lost in familiar surroundings
- boredom – lack of stimulation, activity, exercise
- loss of ability to read or write
- sundowning – leading to lack of rest and quality sleep
- loss of ability to feed oneself – recognize feeding utensils
- loss of attention span –inability to watch television or entertain one's self

ENVIORNMENTAL

- Noise from environment, radio, television, conversation
- Not living at home
- Crowds and commotion
- Excessive hot and/or cold water and air
- Strange or new surroundings
- Too bright or too dark
Strangers

PERSONAL

- Hunger or thirst
- Interruption of normal routine
- Need to use restroom
- Being left alone
- Fear of being abandoned
- Long ride in car
- Inability to communicate, follow instructions, do what you once could
- Loss of ability to respond to whatever is happening around you

CAREGIVER
FAMILY MEMBERS, GUESTS, VISITORS

- Tone of voice
- Improper, rough or abusive handling
- Lack of sensitivity
- Inability to communicate properly
- Asking complex, probing questions that patient is no longer capable of answering
- Not staying in the "here and now" where the patient is

- Being asked to do something you do not understand or you are no longer capable of doing
- Discussing topics that obviously upset the patient

LESSONS LEARNED

- Alzheimer's disease is a degenerative, progressive brain disorder. It is not a mental illness.

- A computer virus and Alzheimer's disease seem to mimic each other.

- The role of a full-time care-partner should be considered an honor and a privilege called to duty rather than volunteering.

- Care-partners change hats like a chameleon changes colors for survival.

- There are at least twenty-one different care-partner hats that should be considered a valuable resource leading toward survival.

- There are many types and sources of anxiety that can often decide how, when, and why the care-partner hats are worn.

- God gives care-partners and their loved ones special years together in spite of the cross that each has to bear.

Chapter 2
DENIAL & DEPRESSION

"Honey, I did an Alzheimer's thing today" (Sarah, 1992)

Allow me to introduce my wife, Sarah P. Schaefer and me, Robert B. Schaefer before I get too involved talking about how denial and depression can affect the average care-partner and victims of the Alzheimer's disease. This book is about Sarah, but it will also look at the range of feelings and emotions that I and other care-partners are likely to experience during such a journey. I cannot overemphasize the fact that this is a story about common, ordinary, and real people facing an incredible trek just as many of you probably will in your own lives.

Sarah was the mother of our four children and grandmother to our eleven grandchildren.

She was my companion, the love of my life, and my best friend. Our story should help you to follow and understand the impact that a diagnosis of probable early onset of Alzheimer's disease, denial, and depression has had upon us, our children, family, and friends. We were average citizens striving to make an honest living. We were not among the rich and famous. Our goal has always been to be successful and self—sufficient.

We realized at the time that Sarah was diagnosed with Alzheimer's that we would never be in a position to afford an assisted living or nursing facility. Long-term care insurance was not available through my employer, until after Sarah was diagnosed; consequently, she was not eligible to purchase it. We have always lived a modest life. To give you an example of where we were financially at the time that we were married, Sarah presented me with four tires for my car, as a wedding present, so that we could relocate to our new residence in upstate New York.

Sarah Eggleston Philbin was born on February 24, 1941 in Forest Hills, N.J. I was born in Floral Park and raised in Douglaston, New York. I met her on a blind date that was arranged by Sarah's best friend at that time. This couple thought that we were the perfect couple. I guess they were right.

Sarah worked as a medical assistant for a family physician and I was about to graduate as a trooper from the New York State Police Academy. That was the beginning of my 35—year career in law enforcement. During the first few months of our courtship, we both spent every dollar of our salaries talking to each other long distance on pay telephones, because I was stationed more than four hours from her home in Forest Hills. There were no cellular telephones with unlimited minutes as we are accustomed to today, in fact, there were no cellular phones. After several months of a pay telephone relationship and weekend dates, we decided to get married. We were actually married eight months after we met. I guess it was love at first sight, if there is such a phenomenon.

Sarah's parents always said that she was attracted to and would someday marry a man who wore a uniform. Sarah was dating a Midshipman at the Naval Academy at the time that we met. In the end, The New York State Police uniform triumphed over that of a Midshipman at the U.S. Naval Academy.

Sarah's parents, Francis and Raphael, are deceased. Raphael was the Sales Manager for the Armed Services Department at National Distillers in New York City and Francis was a stay-at-home mom. Sarah was twenty years old when her father suddenly passed away from heart failure and forty-four at the time of her mother's passing from emphysema. My parents, Frank and Bertha, are deceased. Frank, who died at age 61, was a Latin and Mathematics Professor at Fordham University in the Bronx, New York, following several tours of duty as a Military Police Officer in the U.S. Army. He later became the Secretary for the Civil Service Commission for the City of New York and had the distinction of surviving successfully through the administrations of at least three Mayors for the City of New York. That was an unbelievable feat for anyone. Bertha was the mother of their six children and a full-time stay-at-home mom. Her claim to fame was having had the opportunity in her later years to baby-sit for tennis legend, John McEnroe, when he was an infant. I was twenty-six years old when my father passed away from cancer and thirty-six when my mother passed away from complications following a stroke.

Sarah's older sister and only sibling, Jane, resides in Lynbrook, New York. She is a retired school teacher. I had four brothers and one sister. Brother Frank, the eldest, a career military officer, died from cancer at the age of sixty-two, while Frederic, a speech therapist, died from cancer at the young age of fifty-three. My two surviving brothers are Norbert and John. Norbert, who is retired from the U.S. Air Force, resides in Zephyrhills, Florida. John, a retired Nassau County police officer, resides in Bayville, New York. My only and older sister

Jacqueline, who is retired from Federal Probation, resides in Ft. Myers, Florida. We have not been able to find any history of Alzheimer's or dementia on either side of our families. (Sarah did have an uncle who was said to have been senile, but we never knew much about his condition.)

Sarah has always had an enthusiastic, caring, fun loving, and outgoing personality. She was willing to get involved especially if she could be of assistance to someone else. Sarah was an above average student throughout high school and very popular among her peers because of her outgoing, caring, and likeable personality. She loved children and animals, especially dogs, the outdoors to include the beach, pools and camping, but her first love was always boating. She was raised on her father's boats and could, at any given time, likely be found at or around the helm of a boat.

For those of you who know me now, it will be puzzling for you to learn that as a youngster, I was extremely shy and quiet. I loved the outdoors and boating, but I have always hated the beach and pools. I was an above average student throughout high school. I had few neighborhood and school friends due to being so quiet and shy. I was so shy that I hated any social gatherings. I was horrified at anything having to do with presentations or public speaking. Fortunately, I have overcome or outgrown those fears or quirks over the years. One thing that really stands out in my mind about my youth is the fact that my parents never owned their own home. We were always renters. We were never rich or financially well off, but we lived comfortably.

I must divert for a moment to relate one interesting, exciting and unusual story about Sarah's nautical career, which occurred when she was a freshman in college. It is so representative of her personality and character over the years. Sarah, at the request of her father, cruised their 32—foot Chris Craft, Carolyn, from its mooring in Brooklyn to New York City Harbor. Sarah was to pick up her mother and father and other guests who were attending a bon voyage party for Richard Walters, a family friend, who worked at the United Nations.

Sarah noticed that there was some type of commotion on the pier where she was about to dock her boat. A number of people were frantically waving to her. Initially, Sarah thought that it was her parents and friends, but as she maneuvered into the dock, she realized that she didn't recognize anyone. About the same time that she was ready to ask someone to assist her with the lines of her boat, a young sailor from the cruise ship SS Constitution surprised her by jumping aboard her boat.

Concerned onlookers told her that this crewmember, who spoke little to no English, had missed the sailing of the Constitution seconds before her arrival. The onlookers suggested that Sarah take the sailor out to his ship. The sailor, who was terribly distraught, kept pointing to and mumbling something about the Constitution, which had just left its pier and was still very much in clear view. The onlookers further told Sarah that this sailor had been talking to his mother on the telephone. She was in a New York City hospital. He did not hear the final boarding whistle for the ship and was left behind.

Sarah quickly realized that this sailor would be listed as absent without leave (AWOL) and it probably would have cost him his job with the cruise line. It was ahead full steam as Sarah chased the Constitution in her family boat. It must have been some sight. Sarah quickly caught the Constitution, which seemed to be barely moving. Miraculously, Sarah skillfully pulled close enough to the right side of the Constitution, so that the panicked crewmember could grab and climb up a rope ladder that had been dropped from the side of the ship.

Sarah proudly hit the gas and headed back to the dock where she was to pick up her parents. She was on cloud nine. She could barely wait to tell her father who had just arrived about her good deed. Sarah was shocked to find that this quiet, gentle, but very proud father became very upset as he listened to her story about saving the career of the Constitution seaman. I'm sure that Sarah did not appreciate the accompanying lecture about the severity of the danger that that she had exposed herself and this sailor to by pulling into the wake of such a large ship while it was in motion.

It was a miracle that Sarah and the family boat were not swamped by the Constitution's wake. Her father was not able to reveal his pride in Sarah's performance while he was disciplining her; however, it was revealed in the years that followed, as he recounted her dangerous, but skillful boating adventure that saved the career of a sailor. I am convinced that Sarah would duplicate that dangerous venture today, if she were able to. It didn't matter that Sarah didn't know the individual whom she was helping. It was more about just helping anyone in need. That is the type of person that Sarah was and had always been.

Sarah and I were married after what our parents considered to be a very short courtship. This was a life-changing event for the both of us. We were both super anxious to start our own family. Sarah announced in short order after our marriage that we were expecting our first child. Unfortunately, she had a miscarriage on St. Patrick's Day, March 17, 1964. I will never forget that evening. I happened to be out on patrol at about 7:00pm, when I received a radio transmission to call the state police dispatcher at the barracks. That was never a good sign. I was told to respond to an emergency at my residence.

This required my transporting Sarah to the local hospital at the recommendation of her doctor. Sarah miscarried shortly after our arrival at the hospital.

We were both shattered at the loss of our first child. It was pure agony sitting with Sarah in the hospital because her doctor had somehow led her to believe that she would never be able to have any children. Sarah became more and more depressed during the succeeding months at the thought that she would not be able to have any children. All of her doubts and depression disappeared when our first son Tom was born during March 1965. Sean was born eleven months later during February 1966, Robert Jr. during December 1967 and Kathy February 1973.

Doctors cautioned Sarah that any additional pregnancies could be detrimental to her health and well-being. We were so happy and most appreciative for the beautiful children that we had been blessed with so we didn't dare think about a fifth child. I have often wondered if there could be any connection between the miscarriages and Sarah's early diagnosis of Alzheimer's. In addition to our four children, we have been blessed with eleven beautiful grandchildren to include seven girls and four boys.

Getting back on target, Alzheimer's was a word that my wife Sarah and I never heard or thought much about while we were growing up in New York City. We made it through our teens and into our twenties when we married and began to start a family. We embarked on our careers and quickly moved through our thirties and forties. We may have occasionally heard a reference to senility or hardening of the arteries, but it was not until we were in our late forties that we began to fully understand the true meaning and impact of Alzheimer's disease upon our families and ourselves. Alzheimer's not only destroys the person with the disease, but also affects and may destroy a second victim recognized as a care-partner. It also impacts each and every family member and the circle of friends connected to the victim of this dreaded disease.

Alzheimer's disease sentenced Sarah and I to an indefinite term of denial mixed with varying degrees of depression. It gave us a free ticket to ride on a unique and stressful roller coaster of emotions that continues throughout the progression of this disease. The highs and lows are like nothing that we have ever or will ever experience again in our lives.

1963 – 1987 – Sarah was a stay at home Mom for our 4 children. She worked part-time as a Medical Assistant after all of our children were in school.

The world of denial and depression unofficially started for Sarah and me during 1987-1990. We were relatively new to the Virginia Beach area, where I was transferred following the completion of my assignment at the FBI Academy in Quantico, Virginia.

I do not want to be technical for fear that I lull everyone to sleep. However, I feel that it is necessary to establish a general and loose fitting time-line for the stages of Alzheimer's. Hopefully, by doing that, you will be better able to understand and follow Sarah's progression. I will show Sarah's progression in three stages – the early, middle and late stage.

It is possible for many individuals diagnosed to work and drive during the early stage. It is life as usual with a few short term memory problems and perhaps bouts of misplacing things. Conditions worsen during the middle stage as the activities of daily living begin to deteriorate and in most cases, it will become unsafe for that person to be left alone. During the final stage, the Alzheimer's patient can become totally dependent and usually requires 24/7 care. In many instances, the Alzheimer's patient could become bed-ridden or confined to a wheel chair in the late stage of this disease.

The early stage began for Sarah when she was diagnosed on Dec 18, 1991, although she had been plagued with short term memory loss for several years prior to her diagnosis. Many experts in the field believe that the signs and symptoms of Alzheimer's disease can be traced back as far as 10 years prior to the diagnosis.

Sarah's primary problem before her diagnosis was forgetting along with some minor confusion and misplacement of things. She was capable of working, driving and being left alone. She functioned successfully and safely. Sarah was also capable of responding to an emergency and dialing 911, should that be necessary. I had no reservations whatsoever about leaving her alone or letting her drive. She was still able to handle our financial matters, do the grocery shopping, run errands, do household chores, etc.

Sarah's Alzheimer's progressed gradually to the middle stage. She resigned from her job as a Medical Assistant in September 1993. She voluntarily stopped driving about a month later. Her forgetting and confusion continued to become more and more of a problem. She could perform her activities of daily living, but they were beginning to deteriorate slightly.

We moved to a secure and gated condominium community during 1994, so that I could feel more comfortable about leaving her alone during the day, while I worked. I began to think about retirement during 1995, since I felt that Sarah would be in need of constant supervision for her own safety and well-being. I retired on March 1, 1996 to become Sarah's full-time care-partner.

The final stage became apparent when Sarah was no longer able to perform any of the activities of daily living alone. Sarah's ability to communicate was almost non-existent. She was no longer able to walk or stand on her own. This began to happen following her surgery leading to the removal her gall bladder in 1993. Sarah was able to walk unassisted for about 2 years after her surgery. Eventually, she was confined to a wheelchair or her bed. Sarah was enrolled in hospice for her last two and one half years that she lived in a nursing home.

It seemed like out of nowhere during the period from 1987 – 1990, that Sarah complained daily about short term memory problems, misplacing things and, slight headaches. Our family physician gave her every possible test to rule out any and all of the reversible causes for her short term memory loss. Those included experimenting with possible drug interactions, depression, nutritional losses, thyroid abnormalities, tumors, infections, arteriosclerosis, etc. Tests and scans became the norm until all possible avenues were exhausted. We still didn't have any satisfactory answers to explain her memory loss much less her headaches. This was naturally depressing to Sarah and me, although I tended to make light of it all.

I saw that Sarah was having minor memory problems, but I chose to ignore that because it was just too unpleasant for me to deal with at that time. I tried to rationalize it by assuming that Sarah was probably going through early menopause and perhaps her imagination was getting the best of her. I decided to ignore and/or deny her complaints. It was so much easier for me to engross myself in work, so that I could forget and ignore having to think about or face Sarah's short-term memory loss.

Alzheimer's disease presents itself in clever, shrewd and simple ways. As with most victims, Sarah and I had no idea when and why bits and pieces of her memory were being gnawed away. The early signs and symptoms were subtle and not obvious to Sarah or me and especially to our family and friends. It is much easier now to look back and act as a Monday morning quarterback. I am going to do a little of that to show how blatantly we denied, overlooked and ignored the unceasing and clever work of the identity thief.

Most care-partners and family member with dementia probably do the same either on a conscious or unconscious level. Denial and depression can easily exist for years as it did for the both of us before we recognized and dealt with it properly. By the time Sarah and I recognized and acknowledged what was actually happening, it was almost too late. Alzheimer's was well on its way to achieving victory. The key is to always be proactive. Begin your resource development early within the framework of faith and hope.

I see clearly how I watered down and minimized a number of major incidents that occurred after or just before Sarah received her diagnosis. I was also unconsciously putting pressure on Sarah to deny the obvious truth. We both admitted that unexplained incidents occurred, but we failed to acknowledge the true impact, meaning, or consequences of those incidents. Red flags were waving everywhere. As a new care-partner, I should have but did not see them; or possibly, I chose to ignore them. That was definitely the easiest route that I could have taken. It was equivalent to a buy, buy, buy and worry about paying later state of mind.

We were both protecting ourselves, but as time went on, I as the care-partner began to sense that depression was combining with denial to make matters more critical. The beautiful person that I fell in love with and married was disappearing before my eyes.

I was caring for Sarah at the same time that I was losing her a little bit at a time. I watched her forget who people were. I felt myself grieving the losses. It began as anticipatory grief which was a double-edged sword. I was actually feeling the pain of losing Sarah without her physically disappearing. She was there in body, but her mind and memory were disappearing. I did not share my feelings or emotions concerning Sarah's memory loss with anyone. I became a master at the use of denial. My biggest problem was not wanting to and frankly not being able to face the reality of the situation.

Incident #1 – Boating Accident occurred during 1991

The first incident occurred just prior to Sarah's diagnosis. She, as an experienced boater, made a huge mistake that should have panicked the both of us. We were cruising on Linkhorn Bay in Virginia Beach on a rough and windy day. I was skillfully maneuvering the boat into a gas dock when Sarah perceived that we were in danger of hitting a piling with the rear of our boat. Sarah reacted by using her hand to push away from the piling, thinking that she was preventing damage to the boat. She was holding a new boat-hook in her other hand, but she never used it. That resulted in Sarah severely shattering her wrist. The truth of the matter was that we would not have hit the piling even if Sarah had not attempted to push us off. There was no emergency that necessitated using her bare hand instead of the boat hook. Sarah acted instinctively rather than sensibly. She used poor judgment, which was uncharacteristic of her.

The sound of Sarah's wrist cracking was excruciating. It happened so quickly that I was not able to avoid it. I went to the store at the dock and bought a bag of ice to pack her wrist in, until I was able to transport her to the hospital. She was embarrassed to have made such a mistake. Our brains were not ready and able to accept the severity of the problem that we were facing. It was easier to ignore the obvious. We laughed it off as a stupid and one time mistake. I was quick to use it as an example of what not to do on a boating trip.

I slowly began to recognize that Sarah was having increasing difficulty handling the lines and maintaining her balance, while on the deck of the boat. However, on a conscious and unconscious level, I failed to acknowledge that it was a problem. It was easier to believe that she was having a bad day. I did become angry and frustrated with her instead of dealing with the reality of what I was facing.

It is important early in your career as a care-partner to understand that you will probably resort to anger in situations when you refuse to recognize that you are denying the reasons for your loved ones unexplained or inconsistent behaviors. It is easy to become stuck in yesterday when you fail to acknowledge the obvious. It is easier to expect your loved one to act, behave and perform as they have done in the past. You see what is happening, but you do not want to process it because it is unpleasant. I wanted Sarah to handle events just like she had always done, but that was no longer possible. I saw other changes in Sarah's behavior and performance as my first mate, but denial would not permit me to consciously recognize and do anything about those.

I still did not want to accept it, but it was a beginning. I made a vow to meet this obvious challenge head on. I took a good look at Sarah's recent behavior and convinced myself that there was validity to Sarah's complaints. Denial had been in control up to that point, but I was taking charge again.

December 18, 1991 – Sarah's Initial Diagnosis

It was a cold and windy December 18th, 1991, when Sarah and I reluctantly walked into the office of our neurologist in Virginia Beach, Virginia. This was our official initiation into the world of denial and depression. We had been visiting the same neurologist for a couple years now, but this visit was different for the both of us. Our wedding anniversary was normally a joyous occasion. Somehow, that year we were not in a festive mood. We were extremely apprehensive because we hoped and prayed to put our minds at ease by gaining insight into why Sarah had been plagued by short term memory problems and daily headaches.

Our neurologist seemed to have become tired of our constant grumbling and begging him for a resolution to Sarah's memory problems. We directed a great deal of our frustration, denial and depression toward him. We pressured him to give Sarah her first neurological battery of tests. He did not appear at least on the surface, to be too concerned about her continued memory loss. I guess he felt that tests would establish a baseline to measure further memory loss.

He referred Sarah to the office of Scott W. Sautter, PhD, FACPN on December 4, 1991, at Hampton Roads Neuropsychology, Inc. for testing. Dr. Sautter ordered a neuropsychological battery of tests, to discover why she was consistently plagued by short term memory problems at her young age.

The moment of truth finally arrived for us. I will never forget our neurologist's demeanor that day. He was emotionless, stoic and almost robotic as he looked across his massive desk and read the most important part of Dr. Sautter's report which stated, "The battery of tests indicates that Sarah has the probable early onset of Alzheimer's disease or a related dementia." That statement, as far as we were concerned, was the beginning of the end for the both of our lives as we had known them. We were terrified. Sarah had just been diagnosed with the world's most dreaded disease and the identity thief of the 21st century. Alzheimer's was real to us for the first time. It shattered our limited knowledge of the disease, which included the illusion that it was reserved for the elderly.

We have since been educated. Alzheimer's is not a disease reserved for senior citizens. It can strike anyone, at any age. No one is immune from its ravaging effects. The scariest part of her diagnosis was acknowledging and processing the fact that there are no survivors.

February 12, 1992 – University of Virginia Memory Clinic

Our denial went into overdrive. It partnered with depression and urged us to question the diagnosis. That seemed like the logical and only choice that we had. Denial demanded that we find another reason for Sarah's problems. We badgered our neurologist until he referred us to the Department of Neurology at the University Of Virginia School Of Medicine in Charlottesville, Virginia, on February 12, 1992, for a second opinion. This enabled us to hope that this was a bad dream.

Down deep we knew that the doctors would give us a diagnosis that we could accept and live with. We were convincing ourselves that Alzheimer's disease would not be a reality for Sarah. We were so disappointed when doctors at UVA repeated those terrifying words; "the probable early onset of Alzheimer's disease or a related dementia." However, the doctors said, "But Sarah is so young and she has such a great personality and good sense of humor. The diagnosis doesn't seem to fit." We exhausted ourselves trying to understand what they meant by saying that "the diagnosis doesn't seem to fit." It was contradictory and did not improve our situation. It made us feel that everything was going to be okay.

February, 1992 – Sarah began taking cognex

The doctors at UVA started Sarah in the Cognex access program. Cognex or tacrine was a new Alzheimer's medication in final stage of testing for the Food and Drug Administration (FDA). It was the first cholinesterase inhibitor designed to block the destruction of acetylcholine, which is one of the neurotransmitters in our brains implicated in the chain of chemicals that make up memory. The care-partners of patients who had been involved in testing reported that the cognitive functioning of their loved ones improved while taking it.

Cognex did not cure or stop the progression, but it masked the symptoms for a period of time. What did we have to lose? We both assumed that Cognex would plateau Sarah indefinitely so that we could continue to live normal lives.

The doctor advised us that liver damage was a side effect of Cognex. Sarah took weekly blood tests to monitor her liver function. That was a major inconvenience, but actually was a small price to pay to restore her short term memory. As I think back, I realize that I convinced myself that there was an improvement in Sarah's daily functioning because that is what I wanted to see. Denial did not permit me to see that the medication did little, if anything to improve Sarah's activities of daily living.

Unfortunately, Sarah complained about severe stomach and gastrointestinal discomfort. I tried my best to convince her that it was all in her mind because I wanted this new medication to work. I suggested that she grin and bear it. I was so hoping that she would tolerate the side effects, if I could convince her that Cognex would make her memory problems disappear.

Sarah increased her daily doses of Cognex. The side effects persisted, increased and became more and more annoying. Sarah experienced moderate to severe gastrointestinal reactions, which caused her daily stomach upset, vomiting, diarrhea. Her insides were in constant turmoil. Sarah grew more and more miserable. Her depression increased. The side effects were too much for Sarah to bear. She could barely function with the higher doses of the Cognex and her cognitive functioning continued to decline in spite of this new medication. Any perceived or actual improvements in Sarah's cognitive functioning on my part disappeared quickly or realistically didn't exist in the first place. The doctor decided to keep Sarah on a maintenance dose of

Cognex, since there was no research to indicate if cognitive functioning would decline even more if the Cognex was discontinued.

Sarah and I were upset when Cognex didn't work. We started a rapid descent on the roller coaster of emotions. We tried to increase Cognex again hoping that the side-effects would miraculously disappear. The results were the same. The end result was misery for Sarah. She went back to the maintenance dose of Cognex. We refused to give up the thought of improving Sarah's memory.

Incident #2 – Sarah was issued a Traffic Summons during 1992

Denial reared its ugly head again months later. Sarah and I were working to pack up our house in preparation for the move to a gated condominium community. I was actively addressing Sarah's decline by moving into a gated community, but I was also relying on denial to protect me. The condominium should provide a safer and more secure environment for Sarah, while I was still working, but I was still ignoring early warning signs.

We worked well into the evening hours. At 8:00 pm, I asked Sarah if she would go to one of the nearby fast-food restaurants to get us something to eat. She jumped at the opportunity. I could tell that she wanted a break from the moving nightmare. We were both tired and hungry, but didn't want to give up.

I was so busy that I didn't realize that Sarah had been gone for an hour. Surely there were no lines at the restaurant or traffic at this late hour, but I couldn't figure out what was taking her so long. I thought that she had broken down or been involved in an accident, but if that were the case she would have called me. I decided to give her a few more minutes before going out to look for her.

Another forty minutes passed. I was still working. All of a sudden, Sarah walked in the house. I was just about to scold her for worrying me, when I sensed that she was going to cry. I put on my sensitivity hat, as she reluctantly pulled a piece of yellow paper from behind her back and tearfully announced that the police had given her a summons. I asked her what why she was given a summons. She told that she had been given a summons for forgetting to put her headlights on when she left the parking lot of the fast-food restaurant. I thought that was petty, since I did not recall ever issuing a summons for that when I was a trooper.

Sarah admitted that she was scared because she thought that she might be taken to jail. She told me that the police put on their blue lights and sirens. She recalled that there were at least three or four police cars behind her. They shined spotlights into her windows from the rear of her car. They told her over loud speakers to show her hands and how to get out of her car. The officers had their hands on their guns as they approached. She was sure that she was going to be arrested. The entire incident was terrifying and embarrassing because she didn't have any idea what she had done wrong or why she was being stopped by the police.

The officer's kept asking her questions. They talked on their radios and among themselves for what seemed like an eternity. I began to get more and more upset as Sarah told her story. I thought that it might have been overkill on the part of the officers. As I think back now, I can understand what happened. Sarah forgot to put her headlights on. The police officers attempted to stop her and you can guess what happened. They turned on the blue lights and momentarily Sarah forgot what she was supposed to do.

Mini-Incidents during 1992

August 5, 1992 – Sarah lost her airline ticket in the ladies room at the airport. She was changing planes on the way to visit her sister, Jane in New York. That was Sarah's last trip alone. Fortunately, an airport employee helped Sarah find her ticket and get on her flight without further incident.

August 19, 1992 –Sarah locked her keys in the car with the engine running when she arrived for work. She didn't notice it until the end of her workday. That same day Sarah had difficulty finding her way home from work. She was also unable to deposit money in the bank because she could not recall her PIN.

Sarah took her second Neuropsychological Battery of Tests with Dr. Scott Sautter during October, 1992

Dr. Sautter reported "a slight decrease in almost all areas of cognitive functioning except that she remained unchanged in verbal learning and memory, and immediate recall of narrative verbal material. Interestingly, there was an increase in her abstract concept formation and the ability to think flexibly... She appears to be more aware of the decrease in her cognitive skills and the fact that Cognex did not show dramatic improvements in her abilities...The clinically most significant finding is her increase in depression, which I previously thought was absent." Perhaps there was some improvement that could be attributed to the use of Cognex?

1993 – Mini-Incident during 1993

February 25, 1993 – Sarah had surgery to remove bone from her hip to repair damage caused by her degenerative disc disorder. She was required to wear a cervical collar from that point forward.

Incident #3 – Sarah had difficulty with bank records during 1993

My denial continued to flourish. I received a call from the bank telling that there was a problem with our checking account. It was consistently overdrawn and funds were transferred from our savings account to compensate for the negative balance. Sarah and only Sarah had taken care of our finances and banking records since we were married. She had never had any problems. I didn't understand where the breakdown was – surely it was on the part of the bank because Sarah was perfect with her records. Denial convinced me that Sarah was right and the bank was wrong.

I was never into accounting or bookkeeping. I intentionally avoided figures or accounting. I was too busy with my duties as a Supervisor to handle such trivial matters, or so I thought. I didn't have the time, talent, patience or inclination to deal with our finances. I despised devoting precious time to such drudgery. Sarah volunteered to do the bookkeeping and that pleased me. She had talent in that area and enjoyed it. She juggled our money, figures, and accounts like a magician especially through difficult and lean financial years. That was one less burden on my shoulders.

The call from the bank prompted me to look at latest check register. I wanted to prove that Sarah was doing fine. I did it discretely so that Sarah would not know about it. I found one register. It didn't have many entries and the ones that were there didn't make much sense. The addition was wrong or incomplete and there were numbers crossed out or written over. It was a mess. Sarah was forgetting to make entries and her calculations were awful. I couldn't believe what I saw. She had no idea that she was having a problem, or at least she didn't want to admit it. I know that I didn't want to admit it either. It was way too big for either of us to be able to absorb and digest.

Denial permitted us to mask the importance of this and the previous incidents on a conscious and unconscious level. These incidents combined with Sarah's daily complaints of forgetting still did not completely resonate with either of us. I believe that we knew that we were in trouble, but our minds were not capable of accepting the full impact of Alzheimer's disease. I was stuck in yesterday wanting Sarah to be like she had been rather than what she was becoming.

The banking incident got my attention. It was an awakening for both of us. I forced myself to acknowledge something was wrong and I needed to meet it head on before it was too late. Sarah's memory was failing and we had reached the point that we could no longer use denial to protect us. Some of my investigative expertise probably kicked in and helped to bring me to the point that I wanted to face reality.

Incident #4 – Sarah was experiencing difficulty at work during 1993

I decided to call Sarah's office manager at the surgeon's office where she was a medical assistant. I was dumbfounded when her office manager and friend broke down crying. She was relieved that I had called her. She related that she had been trying to get up the nerve to call me and to tell me that Sarah was having difficulty with her work. Memory loss was interfering with everything that Sarah did at work. She put off calling me because she didn't want to hurt Sarah's or my feelings.

Over the past several months, Sarah's work performance deteriorated significantly. She had trouble concentrating and remembering. It reached the point that Sarah was no longer able to cover up her mistakes. Her job involved scheduling patients and surgeons for procedures at Virginia Beach Hospital. Apparently, Sarah would schedule a surgeon for a procedure and forget to schedule a patient for the same procedure or vice versa.

Her office manager admitted that within the last week she looked out the window when Sarah left for the day. Sarah exited the parking lot and turned to the right instead of to the left which was her way home. She immediately turned to the right again made a u-turn and sat on a dead-end street for an hour. Sarah was disoriented and appeared to be figuring out which way she should turn to get home. Her watching rather than helping Sarah and her reluctance to call me about her difficulties indicated that denial also affected her office manager. No one is immune from denial when a tragedy or other unpleasant situation occurs.

Denial and depression can be contagious. They can manipulate others connected to the victims of memory loss, especially when early onset is involved. It is difficult to accept memory problems at any age, but it is so much more painful to swallow when the victim is as young as Sarah was when she was diagnosed. The previously mentioned incidents combined with my conversation with Sarah's office manager and her continued complaints of forgetting whittled my denial.

Mini-Incidents Continue during 1993

Testing at John Hopkins University Memory Clinic on 12/12/93
Residual denial prompted me to continue to seek a better and more pleasant explanation for Sarah's memory loss. We went to the Department of Neurology at John Hopkins University Medical School in Baltimore, Maryland, on December 12, 1993 for a third opinion. Surely this time, the doctors at John Hopkins would discover something new which would permit us to solve Sarah's memory problems and get us back to leading a normal life. There must be some other answer. All we had to do was find it. Denial was going out of its way to help us to find a solution that would be more pleasing and acceptable

Once again, we were shocked and devastated when the doctors at John Hopkins repeated, the same words—the probable early onset of Alzheimer's or a related dementia; however, they also said, "Sarah is so young. She has a great personality and good sense of humor. It doesn't seem possible" We continued to be confused. It seemed as if the doctors at UVA and John Hopkins did not trust their own test results and diagnosis probably because of Sarah's age. That left us hanging in again mid-air.

Testing at Department of Neurology, Eastern Virginia Medical School on February 19, 1995

Those words spoken by the doctors at UVA and John Hopkins haunted and prompted us to go one step further. We went to Department of Neurology at Eastern Virginia Medical School (EVMS) for an unprecedented fourth opinion. I am not sure what prompted us to go this far, but we were committed to finding a new start for Sarah.

We were overwhelmed when we received the diagnosis from the doctors as EVMS. It read as follows: "With the benefit of this comprehensive evaluation and past test data, it is clear that Mrs. Schaefer is experiencing ongoing cognitive decline of a generalized higher cortical nature. Memory impairment is accompanied by deficits in reasoning through new problems and particular difficulty with spatial motor skills. She is now showing at least moderate dementia...a dementia process of this type is consistent with, but certainly not limited to, early onset Alzheimer's disease." Those words still echo in my mind. This time that doctor recommended that Sarah stop driving. Fortunately, Sarah had previously agreed to stop so that was not a problem. This was the first time that anyone had approached that with us. It was another sign that we needed to take begin to face the reality of Alzheimer's disease. Denial was not going to be able to help us any longer.

We plummeted to an all time low. This time the doctors did not add any comments about Sarah's personality or sense of humor. We did not want to discuss Sarah's diagnosis with anyone. We weren't interested in educating ourselves about it either. We wanted to keep the diagnosis a secret, but that was impossible. We were scared. That fear was followed by a cycle of intense and overwhelming feelings and emotions to include, but not limited to emptiness, disbelief, anger, sadness, embarrassment, numbness, pessimism, fatigue, confusion, loneliness, and devastation. I could see that Sarah was depressed as she became more and more aware that there was definitely something wrong with her memory, but I didn't know how to make that better.

Better versus Bitter

I was fortunate that much of my professional law enforcement career centered in the areas of stress management, critical incidents and peer support. That knowledge and experience helped me to cope with and eventually better overcome the denial and depression that I faced. I was able to recover, pick up the pieces and motivate myself to become a survivor rather than a second victim. These skills equipped me with the ability to guide and protect Sarah as we moved through the world of Alzheimer's together.

I taught Sarah from day one that she should use the comic defense. That is a favorite coping technique in my bag of stress management tricks. In a stressful situation, rely on the comic defense for help and relief. Put your strength and energy into finding something positive or funny in every negative situation. Out of the dirt, laughter allows us to cope with the human condition. Rid yourself of the negativism and replace it with something positive. That is the only way to survive. It shuts down the stress reaction at least momentarily and gives you an opportunity to rejuvenate and restore balance. This is difficult because it requires prayer, strength, willpower, time and energy.

Sarah was a quick learner. Every time she caught herself forgetting or making a mistake, she would quickly and proudly announce, "Honey, I did an Alzheimer's thing today." She would then tell me about one of her Alzheimer's incidents. We had a good laugh about it. That gave us the break in the stress reaction that we both needed. We were then ready to wage our full-time battle toward survival. Such feedback helped me to gauge exactly where Sarah was at any given time in her progression. I could then make necessary and appropriate changes to assure for her safety and well-being.

I arrived home from work one evening at 6:30 pm. It was unusual that Sarah was waiting for me as I pulled into the garage. She was so excited. She couldn't wait until I got out of the car. She rushed to me and blurted out, "Honey, I did an Alzheimer's thing today". I greeted her and tried to calm her down, but that was impossible. Sarah continued, "I arrived at work at 9:00 am today and parked in my usual space. I locked the car and went into the office. I returned at 1:30 pm because today was a half-day. When I got to the car, I realized that I had locked my keys in the car." I asked how she got home. She said, "The office manager drove me home so that I could pick up my spare keys." I told her that that was nice of her office manager so I would pick up flowers or fresh cookies at the bakery and drop them off tomorrow. Sarah quickly continued, "But, honey, that's not all of it. The engine ran for the entire time." We both sat down and had a hardy laugh and forgot about the incident.

Denial helped me to put that incident on the back burner because I remember doing a similar thing myself. I accidently locked the doors of my state police car while the keys in the ignition and the car idling. To make matters worse, it was during a blinding snow storm and I had a prisoner in handcuffs that I was taking to a magistrate. I justified Sarah's incident by saying that it happens to everyone.

During my critical incident classes, I have always taught the victims of a crisis that they will face an important and difficult decision that involves choosing between becoming bitter or better. Only they can make that choice. It sounds simple, but it requires an untold amount of thought, time and energy to overcome bitterness in favor of becoming better. Bitterness is the easiest route because it requires zero time and effort. Sit back and relax and let the bitterness take over your life and your decision making. At that point, you will have lost control and be on the way to failure and disaster. Better, on the other hand, is much more difficult, but is equivalent to survival.

I wanted so much to be a survivor and so did Sarah, although the odds were against us both. The road to survival is not the easiest route. It is loaded with curves and obstacles. Within a year or two of Sarah's diagnosis, I took one giant step toward survival when I, reached out and made my first contact with the Southeastern Chapter of the Alzheimer's Association. I was a bit skeptical about getting help from anyone, but fortunately, something pushed me. That was a major turning point in my life and in my ability to survive and move through the denial and depression stage.

I received tons of information about Alzheimer's and dementia. The next thing you know, I was a volunteer, a member of their speaker's bureau and a member of the Board of Directors. I became the Chair for the Patient and Family Services Committee, involved in Memory Walk and volunteered to write articles about care-partners struggling with dementia. I volunteered to teach Alzheimer's/dementia topics to care-partners and first responders. I was active spreading the word, especially about the early onset of Alzheimer's. If you want to feel good about yourself—do something for someone else. That is what I have done and what Sarah attempted to do as long as she was able to during her progression. My intent has always been to make something positive out of a very negative situation. It has enabled me to cope better and to progress through the stages of a care-partners development.

LESSONS LEARNED

• A traumatic incident may occur at any time to any of our loved ones.

• A diagnosis of Alzheimer's disease is a traumatic incident.

• There is no cure for Alzheimer's disease nor is there any medication that will stop its progression.

• Sarah & Bob Schaefer are common and ordinary people.

• Sarah was diagnosed with the probable early onset of Alzheimer's disease or a related dementia, while she was still in her forties.

• Bob was drafted into the role of full-time care-partner.

• Alzheimer's/dementia strike its victims without regard to age, race, color, and creed.

• Avoid becoming stagnant or stuck in this or any step of development as a care-partner.

• Reach out early to family, friends, clergy, physician, emergency room, elder attorney, and organizations such as the Alzheimer's Association, etc. for help and support.

• Listen to your body when the signs of stress become evident. Monitor the signs and symptoms of depression.

• Practice stress management as a lifestyle rather than a passing fancy to guarantee, growth, maturity, and successful passage through the steps of development as a care-partner.

Chapter 3
RESENTMENT MIXED WITH ANGER

Sarah said on 3/27/97, "I'm in a different world and I don't think I'll ever find the other."

Resentment is the second stage of development that the average care-partner will likely face. It could be mixed with some anger at times. As with all of the stages, it is difficult to set hard fast rules or specific timelines for development and duration. This happens because we are individuals with differing perceptions, upbringing and backgrounds. As such, we will react differently as we face a crisis and attempt to survive the accompanying aftermath.

My resentment began during 1992-3, while I was still heavily involved in the turmoil caused by the denial and depression stage. Resentment gathered for a number of years. I believe that all of the stages of development will overlap to some degree. Occasionally, they will disappear and surface again for short periods of time, especially while you are stressed. I do not believe that any of the milestones will ever totally disappear until you reach peace of mind.

Let me focus on Sarah during 1994. This will help to see the more obvious changes as they began occurring in her progression.

On 5/23/94, Sarah said, "I felt like I was having a stroke or something when I played bridge last night. I couldn't remember anything."

On 7/25/94, it was too risky to leave Sarah at home alone, while I was working full-time. I decided to move to a condominium in a gated community. I thought that would be good for the both of us. I would feel more comfortable about leaving Sarah home alone in that environment. She needed a security code to go or do anything. I convinced myself that there would be no danger of her getting lost or into any trouble while she was alone. There was a maintenance worker and housekeeper available days who agreed to watch out for her.

I realized that Sarah's ability to reason or solve problems deteriorated to the point that everything required total concentration. She could only do one thing at a time. Her conversations wandered all over the place. She was hesitant to talk on the telephone, especially if she was asked to give directions to a realtor who wanted to show our house. Sarah was not able to make change at the yard sale that she insisted on having before we moved to the condo.

On 8/1/94, we moved into the Cove Point Condominiums in Virginia Beach, VA.

On 9/7/94, Sarah wanted to withdraw $120 from an ATM. She was not able to complete the transaction. A line built up behind her so she left without getting any money. She returned and was able to withdraw $100. She was totally lost because she had to withdraw money in multiples of 10. That was too much for her to understand on that day.

Resentment begins with the unresolved anger that often follows a major negative event or crisis in life. In a sense, you feel unreasonably victimized. This happens with diagnosis of Alzheimer's or dementia because it is such a horrendous and feared disease. It may begin and be masked by denial. Anger joins the mix and leads to hatred, cynicism and sarcasm. Care-partners can easily get stuck in the resentment stage, which over time leads to discomfort. Care-partners should be proactive to overcome and manipulate the denial, depression, resentment and anger that naturally appear and attempt to dominate them.

When Sarah's memory problems first began to appear, I was not very sensitive. That naturally raised Sarah's resentment level, although she didn't let it be known. I treated Sarah's complaints as if they were exaggerated and even unfounded. I was so absorbed in my career that I had little time or sensitivity left for anything else. I didn't have the time or the patience to listen to Sarah's complaints. She was tolerant of my shortcomings and we remained a happy couple.

We were actually having the time of our lives. We lived in a beautiful condominium community on the water a mile and a half from the oceanfront. We were not able to see the ocean from our deck, but we could see some of the hotels on what was called 'the strip.' All of a sudden, Alzheimer's appeared and disrupted our lives. That naturally touched off a lot of emotions for the both of us.

The relentless forgetting and headaches led to numerous daytime telephone complaints while I was at work. These eventually moved to the evening hours whenever I tried to relax. It was impossible to talk to the kids, read the newspaper or watch television. Sarah repeated the same things over and over again, night after night. It reached the point that I told Sarah to take a Tylenol and rest to make her headache disappear. I thought that her memory might improve if she could stop the headaches. I finally told her to stop complaining. I thought that she might be a hypochondriac because if her memory was that bad, how could she remember to complain about the same things day after day, and night after night? I wanted to ignore her, but I was not able to. I wanted to deny that there was a problem.

It is difficult to imagine what Sarah was going through herself during that same period of time. I wanted to be sensitive, but I wasn't. My sensitivity needed some fine tuning. I also tried to laugh at the memory loss hoping that it would go away. When all else failed, I reminded Sarah that she was getting older and that her problems were probably due to normal aging. As a last resort, I lost my temper and lashed out saying that I could not solve her problem. I told her to talk to a doctor. She let me know that she had been going to the doctor, but he seemed to be puzzled about her memory loss.

Sarah persisted with marathon visits to her family physician who gave her test after test in an effort to get to the root of her problem. This continued for years without any suitable resolution. I wanted to believe that it was all in Sarah's mind, but the evidence was mounting that Sarah was forgetting. Denial is common at and after a diagnosis of dementia, but it can appear and reappear during the progression.

Care-partners be cautious and understand that resentment can take over lives and change them for the worse just like denial has a tendency to do. All too often, a mindset develops that causes you to challenge everything. It can be disruptive and lead you toward negativism. Examples of these thoughts patterns might include—What did I do to deserve this? What did Sarah do to deserve this? Why can't things be like they were? Why am I or we being singled out for such punishment? Where is this disease going to take me—Us? How are we going to afford this? What is happening to me – Us? – Where is my family?— Where are all my friends? – Why can't I do anything?

It seems like life isn't fun anymore? Sarah cannot follow instructions or do anything by herself. She has no long or short term memory at all. Why can't I go anyplace? I do not have a life any longer!" These questions don't have satisfactory answers, but yet we beat our heads against a wall trying to answer them. They are constantly on your mind. It becomes difficult to find a way or reason to keep fighting such a losing battle. The unanswered questions, the demands, and the stress accumulate. It seems natural to turn bitter and resent everything and everyone. The easiest thing to do is wallow away in your own self-pity. I would not permit that to happen, but I was not sure where to turn to help myself. In the early stage, Sarah was right at my side waging her battle against bitterness and resentment, but they tend to come naturally.

I had to constantly remind myself of the bitter or better concept during every stage of my development to help to maintain a positive attitude. That idea turns some people off. I have talked to care-partners who have told me that bitter or better was not an option for them. They believe that they are and have always been negatively charged. They are predisposed to being negative. That type of thinking will lead to the easy way out, failure and bitterness. It is much easier to give in and become negative because it requires zero effort. I've heard it said that average people take the easy way out of difficult situations. That is a cop-out. I do not believe that even though it is more difficult to take the positive route. It took every ounce of energy on my and Sarah's part to continually be positive; however, we made the right choice and it paid off. You need super-strength and determination. It is not too big of a monster to conquer. We would not let ourselves think that; if you want a helping hand, look at the end of your arm. That might seem overly simplified, but it is true. Sink as a victim of the identity thief, or make the choice to swim for survival. If you do not know how to swim then learn very quickly through trial and error. The key is to adapt to this and every stressful situation that you encounter in your life.

This is a perfect time to reassess. Where are you? Are you counting your blessings as well as the hardships that tend to overshadow them? Are you keeping things in proper prospective? Succumbing to the negative and ignoring the positive is a certain recipe for disaster. Attitude is the key to overcoming adversity.

Sarah and I have always loved life and had a tremendous desire to be survivors, in spite of the odds. We have experienced our share of ups and downs. Alzheimer's disease is serious and life threatening. It is a major challenge. I have been asked often how I survived so many years as a care-partner. I emphasized that I overcame major obstacles by generating and displaying a positive attitude mixed with faith and love, patience, and a sense of humor. Sarah's inner strength and very being have also been so, so powerful in motivating and strengthening me on my long journey. Sarah taught me valuable and priceless lessons along the way.

Sarah and I participated in a television special while we were living in the Tidewater area of Virginia. This program was titled, Gray Matters – Issues in Aging. We were more than willing to participate to create something positive out of our negative situation. This same attitude helped us to overcome the denial, depression, frustration and anger that we encountered on a daily basis. It was our bitter or better attitude at work. I will share this brief program with you so that you will again have an appreciation of Sarah's performance during the middle stage of her progression. She did well and you could see that personality and sense of humor that the doctors referred to earlier.

GRAY MATTERS – ISSUES IN AGING
WVEC-TV & Sentara Health System
12/18/95

Sarah said, "I wanna be what I was. I'm losing it."

Bob said, "When we received the initial diagnosis it turned out to be our anniversary. And it was kind of a shattering experience the early onset of Alzheimer's or a related disease. A little bit of denial set in and as a result of that, we've been to several of the major hospitals and universities for a follow up diagnosis all of which have come out the same."

The commentator said, "And there's no denying the symptoms."

Sarah said, "It's a lot of forgetful. I mean if you compare you to me I forget 2 minutes after I say it. I forget what I've said. I get frustrated a lot. You know I I'll want to say something and it just won't come out and thank goodness I've got him as my support because he usually can read my mind and continue when I start something and I say well I've just lost it.

Bob said, "It's a tough situation. I know that it's not her fault, but at times she's not herself. It's one of those situations when you talk about coping you can get angry and you can become bitter or you create a lot of everyday memories that she'll have to remember. And that's what I've chosen to do as opposed to get angry at it.

The commentator said, "Although Bob misses the way things were during their 32 year marriage he said it hasn't put a strain on their love for one another."

Bob said, "I think if anything it's probably increased it. It's made me more attentive to everyday of life. I think of a lot of things I took that for granted as she raised the four children a lot of times I think on her own. Gradually, I'm taking over a lot of those responsibilities such as the checkbook, and the grocery shopping we do together. I find us doing a lot more things together which we probably should have been doing all along. When I leave for work in the morning I leave a little to do list with things she might do during the day to prevent her from being bored and isolated and feeling confined."

The commentator said, "Sarah can't venture too far from home anymore. It's no longer safe for her to drive."

Bob said, "I wasn't really taking her keys away. She still has her keys. Sarah – laughing –interrupted – "But I can't find them." Bob continued –"She voluntarily agreed not to drive the car. We decided to meet this head on."

Sarah said, "But, I can't find them (laughing)."

Sarah participated in a second presentation two years later at Hampton University. She was asked to speak about her diagnosis at an education conference for the Southeastern Chapter of the Alzheimer's Association. Sarah agreed by saying, "I will do it if it will help someone else."

She performed okay for the interview, but it took every bit of strength and energy that she could muster up. She was not able to do anything else for the remainder of that day.

I was at her side whenever she did anything, especially if it involved one of the activities of daily living. I tried discretely to let her do whatever she could on her own without my assistance. That was important to her. I did not want to embarrass her, so I gave hints and clues along the way. That coaching and prompting went a long way, but it was not easy.

Looking at the content of this presentation should give a good idea of how Sarah was thinking and feeling at the time. I prepared Sarah for weeks in advance. I hoped that the rehearsals would make it easier for her on the day of her presentation. Sarah did well when we practiced the questions and answers at home. I prepared three questions and I wrote down the answers that Sarah had given during those practice sessions. The answers were all in Sarah's own words.

HAMPTON UNIVERSITY—AUGUST 9, 1997

Bob said, "Sarah, I have a couple of additional questions maybe to give you all a little more insight and the first question—Sarah, what was your reaction to a diagnosis of the probable early onset of Alzheimer's disease ?"

Sarah answered, "I was scared and I did not believe the diagnosis. I went to the University of Virginia, uh Johns Hopkins University and Eastern Virginia Mili… uh, Medical School and uh nobody could say that there was anything they could do. Uh and a… they gave us some medications. None of the medications really worked—if they worked they worked for a little bit or they didn't work at all and now there's not anything and uh (unintelligible). I have a beautiful support group with my family. They're around all the time for me. And a…

Bob asked, "That's jumping into the second question that I was gonna ask is—How have you been able to cope with everyday life?"

Sarah answered, "It's been a little hard because I'm used to being— I was a medical assistant for many years and it's kind of hard to sit back and make your spouse have to feed you—not feed you— I'm not that far bad, hopefully. Uh, but he does the dishes, he—I do clean the house a little bit, but I never did that too well anyways— (laughs). So (pause) and oh the cooking—I'm sorry, he does all the cooking too (laughs). Uh—oh yes, and we have four kids that are very, very supportive to us and if Pops has to be away or something like that—they make sure that somebody's around. (Long pause)"

Bob asked, "Okay then, I'm sure she is glad to hear this—the final question, what message would you like to give to this audience?"

Sarah answered, "Please remember Alzheimer's in your prayers – and hope that we can correct this disease (long pause)."
Bob said, "And that's it."

I learned during this presentation that Sarah had difficulty reading. In fact, I do not think that she was able to read the answers at all, especially because she was stressed about making the presentation. The answers were typed in bold print, but she didn't seem to be able to read them. That is why she hesitated and stuttered and stammered more toward the end of her talk. This helped me to recognize that Sarah was not doing as well as I thought that she was at the time, but she was skilled at hiding her failings from me.

The following are the questions and answers that we rehearsed. Once again, this should give you an idea of how the identity thief was affecting Sarah's performance.

What was your reaction to a diagnosis of the probable early onset of Alzheimer's disease?

I was scared and did not believe the diagnosis. I went to the University of Virginia, John's Hopkins and Eastern Virginia Medical School. The results were all the same. It was a gradual – losing things and not remembering what I had said five minutes ago. I lose track of thoughts. I can't remember from one thing to another. I am not as outgoing as I was before. I do not jump into things like I use to. Things constantly come and go for me.

How have you been able to cope with everyday life?

I have a great support system in my family. I can do some things without my husband, but I might do them wrong. Our daughter lives in the local area. She is very supportive and goes out of her way to take me out and do things together. Our three sons live in Richmond. We don't see them as often, but they are supportive and helpful. They look out for me. We as a couple always try to be positive, laugh a lot and take one day at a time.

What message would you like to give to this audience?

Please remember all Alzheimer's patients in your prayers and continue to work and pray hard for a cure for this terrible disease.

We did not feel much resentment at the time of Sarah's diagnosis. That was due in part to the fact that we were overrun with denial. Resentment reared its ugly head when I recognized that the good life was slipping away. At the same, I was working twenty-four hours a day—seven days a week. I lost control of my life and everything around me. I had to fight with all my might to keep a positive attitude. I reinforced my personal commitment to prevent the flame from going out. Support groups and the constant theme of doing something for someone else helped the both of us to keep our heads above water as we navigated through the rough waters during the first and second milestones.

I was forced to retire from my dream job as an FBI agent to be Sarah's full-time care-partner. I could also find full-time caregivers for her at home. The only other alternative would be to place Sarah in a long-term facility, but I would not to do that. That was a no, no because I promised her that I would keep her at home for the duration of her illness. Care-partners should be careful about making such promises. Alzheimer's will progress and the care of your loved one will become more and more complex. Care could easily progress beyond your capabilities. Understand there is no shame or embarrassment in placing your loved one in a nursing home. Care-partners tend to be extremely hard rather than patting themselves on the back for a job well-done.

Constant repetition will wear the best and most patient care-partners out. Sarah and I always celebrated the 4th of July at the lake house of her relatives in S.C. On 7/3/96, my resentment level rose significantly when Sarah lost her glasses while swimming. She was not able to see well without her glasses. Unfortunately, I was not smart enough to bring a spare set. She was fixated with diving for her glasses. The repetition was non-stop. I was afraid to let her dive, so I asked one of her cousins to do the diving. He searched for hours, but the glasses were nowhere to be found. Sarah kept harping on the fact that she could find her glasses, if only I let her dive for them. That was out of the question. It was far too dangerous for her to dive. Every time I turned my back, Sarah tried to sneak back to the lake. It reached the point that Sarah asked me what she was looking for. She forgot that she had lost her glasses, but she remembered that she had to search for something. That was frustrating and upsetting. She was so obsessed with the loss of her glasses that I drove her home that night. The repetition never ended. I resented that and the fact I had to cut our vacation short because of her glasses. Alzheimer's continued to disrupt our lives with similar incidents.

I tried to ignore that resentment was building because of those incidents. They happened more and more frequently. At the same time, I was taking over more and more chores and responsibilities. Sarah's care was becoming more difficult. We always shared responsibilities during our marriage. Now, I am doing the grocery shopping, laundry, cleaning, cooking, menu planning, budget, checkbook, house and yard maintenance, car maintenance, and feeding and walking the dog. Sarah was no longer able to do things even with simple instructions. That was distressing for Sarah and me. She knew that something was happening to her, but she wasn't sure what it was. It bothered me because I, as a male, was not accustomed to doing so many of those things that I had to do, not to mention Sarah's personal care. It seemed unfair, but there was nothing I could do about it. Resentment naturally flourished in that type of an environment.

Resentment increased even more when I realized that everything that we loved and cherished disappeared and we had no control over that. I was forced to sell my dream boat. That was the same boat that we planned to use to cruise the inland waterway after my retirement. Boating was far too dangerous for Sarah. I sold our dream condominium that we had only lived in for a little over four years. Everything was hazardous for Sarah.

An example happened on a freezing February day when I had to stop Sarah from jumping into the frigid waters of the bay adjacent to our condo to rescue our dog. I tried to rationalize moving by saying that it would be advantageous to be closer to our children who lived in the Richmond area, so that they might be able to assist me with Sarah's care in the future.

I felt as if I was under house arrest. Sarah would not let me out of her sight. I had to watch and help her with everything that she did or tried to do. I was on call 24 hours a day, seven days a week in law enforcement, but this was so much more intense and demanding. When I worked a major case, I knew that the stress would end after hours, days, weeks or possibly months, at the worst. The stress of working with Sarah and her Alzheimer's never went away. That is what makes the job of care-partner so unique, demanding, and stressful. As the disease progresses, so too do your responsibilities and the stress that naturally accompanies them. New challenges appear daily. Stress and the workload increase, while peace and quiet and rest and relaxation vanish.

I did everything with and for Sarah. I had little if any help which bothered me. My personal life, friends, interests and hobbies were gone. I did not have time to do anything, but take care of Sarah. I did not have the time or inclination to even take care of myself. I convinced myself that I did not want or need help from anyone. At the same time, I was bitter and resented that no one wanted to help me with this unbelievably stressful task. It was lonely because Sarah was losing her ability to have any meaningful conversations and no one visited us anymore. It was a lonely existence. I was annoyed that everyone disappeared.

Sarah said repeatedly, "Do you know what? I love you." That was her favorite thing to say for months. She repeated it over and over again to the point that it drove me crazy. She also frequently asked, "If anything happens to me will you get married again?" She asked that day and night. She even suggested who I should marry after she died. She was genuinely concerned about me and wanted to be sure that I was taken care of, if anything happened to her. I insisted that I was not interested in marrying again. I emphasized that I would always be there to take care of her and she would not be going anyplace because I was taking such good care of her. I reassured her that I would always be by her side and there would be no need for me to remarry.

Bob made a major decision during 1997 concerning a very sensitive and taboo topic.

We were still able to have sex on a very, very limited basis up to this year. It was infrequent over the last few years due to my personal feelings and quirks. I felt awkward thinking about it, much less doing it. It was a sensitive issue that kept me awake nights. I was Sarah's full-time care-partner. I was also her husband, but that seemed secondary to my role as a care-partner. It was a major case of role conflict that confused and distressed me. I did not understand how I, as Sarah's care-partner could think about having sex with her. It just didn't seem right. I felt that I was taking advantage of her. My role as a care-partner was more of a professional relationship that did not include a sexual relationship. I felt that I was taking advantage of her because she did not fully understand or realize exactly what is happening. She was lost in everything that she did and sex was no different. Sarah was so easy going and wanted to please me, but at the same time I don't think that she could give her consent any longer. She was increasingly scared, anxious and paranoid. I feared that if I continued to have sex under those circumstances, it could border on abuse and I did not want any part of that. It was a difficult decision as a man, but I felt that it was best not to continue to have sex with her. I didn't anticipate having to make that decision, but I was concerned about forcing myself on her. Sarah never said a word about it, and we never discussed it; however, again, I sensed that it was a relief for her because she was no longer able to understand or complete the act and process the accompanying feelings and emotions. Continued sex might possibly cause her to retreat even further into her world that I did not want. On a positive note, I began to better appreciate that under those circumstances, we could continue to show our love, devotion and affection in different ways. A smile, hug, kiss, holding hands or just being with her on the good days as well as the bad ones was a better alternative to my dilemma.

The following situations should give you a better picture of Sarah's confusion and disorientation, as I was working my way through the trials and tribulations of the resentment stage.

Sarah began using Aricept on 2/7/97.

On 2/8/97, I picked out an outfit that Sarah could wear to church the next morning and out to dinner that same evening. I do that a day in advance because it takes so long for me to get her dressed. I was not able not find an outfit that pleased her. She found fault with anything and everything. I was frustrated and lost my temper. How much can any one person possibly take?

She disappeared into her own world. I felt bad, but it was too late. Fortunately, Sarah forgot about my angry outburst in a couple hours and we were back to normal. She also forgot about the outfits, so we started over again. This time she agreed to wear one of the outfits. Later that same evening Sarah said, "I am sorry for being so much trouble." That comment broke my heart. I was angry at her and she is apologizing. I vowed to do better and not lose my temper. I had to acknowledge and harness my resentment before it built up. I was lazy and taking shortcuts. I knew that Alzheimer's was causing her to act the way that she did. It was not intentional on her part. She was as helpless as I was. I realized that I had to change because Sarah was no longer able to change.

On 2/14/97, Sarah tried to empty the dishwasher. She took a spatula out and said, "What is this?" I thought to myself, my God, she is struggling to remember anything at this point. Later that same day Sarah kept asking, "Who am I. Where am I going?"

On 2/21/97, Sarah said, "Do you love me as I am? I'm losing it. I can't do anything anymore."

On 2/23/97, Sarah asked over and over again, "How old am I going to be tomorrow?" I told her she was going to be 56. She was convinced that I was kidding. She kept saying, "I am not 56 – I am not that old. You are kidding me." I was not able to convince her that she was going to be 56, so I finally just backed off and told her that she was only 39. She was happy with that and there was peace once again. It is a constant battle to remember not to argue and to go with the flow.

On 2/25/97, Sarah said – "How old am I?" I told her that she was 56. Sarah said, "Oh, I'd rather be fifty-one." Later that same day Sarah said, "I'm getting worser."

On 2/28/97, I was feeling sorry for myself and alone because of Sarah's decline. No one knows or appreciates what I am going through. I always discussed my problems, feelings and emotions with Sarah, but that is no longer possible. Now, I have no one to talk to. I am very lonely. Everyone seems to doubt me and thinks that I am overreacting. I'm trying not to be paranoid, but that is the how I feel. I am frustrated and resentful. Spend several days alone with Sarah and all of those doubts will disappear. Seeing her for a couple of hours is misleading because she covers-up so well for short periods of time. I know that I am solely responsible for Sarah's care; however, I would feel better if others understood how difficult this was. I'm not sure what I want or what I'm looking for, so I will continue to do what I have been doing. I can do this forever.

On 3/15/97, I just wanted to run away. I know its not Sarah's fault, but I am stressed. I am losing my temper more often. I am snapping at Sarah. It doesn't happen often, but I have to stop myself from getting upset and losing my temper. It is not doing either of us any good. God bless Sarah. She knows that something is going on with me, but she has no idea that she is causing it. She has enough memory left to want to help me solve my problems. She is so eager to please me. She knows that I am doing it all. She feels inadequate. She tries to fold laundry, empty the dishwasher, empty the garbage, and walk the dog; however, at times, it is more trouble to let her do those chores. I have to stop what I am doing and walk her slowly through every step of what she is doing. I want her to continue to help me because I know that that is best for her, but it is becoming more and more difficult and time consuming.

On 3/17/97, Sarah said,—"Take me out into the ocean and dump me. I can't go on."

On 3/22/97, at 6:25pm, Sarah said, "I'm in a different world and I don't think I'll ever find the other. Why don't you take me and drop me into the ocean. I can't do anything. I can't do anything at all. I am useless."

On 3/22/97, I must make a major decision that is not to my liking. It is unsafe for Sarah to assist me on the boat. She is not able to handle the lines any longer. I am afraid that she will fall overboard or injure herself. She does not remember the front of the boat from the rear or the left from the right. She frightens the daylights out of me. We have almost had a couple disasters because Sarah did not understand and/or process what I was saying. I do not have the nerve to tell her that I am selling the boat because of her condition. It is killing me, but I have the boat up for sale. It will be a disaster if Sarah found out that I sold the boat because of her Alzheimer's. She knows how much I enjoy it and so does she; however, it is my only option now. I made up a flimsy excuse about it being too expensive and my losing interest in it. Thank goodness she didn't question my motives because that would have made it even more difficult. We have hardly been able to use the boat this season because of my fears about Sarah hurting herself or drowning.

On 3/30/97, I was talking on the telephone and wishing a member of our family a Happy Easter. I gave the telephone to Sarah. Somehow, she disconnected the call several times. I got angry again and yelled out that I couldn't take this anymore. Sarah disappeared immediately. I felt guilty when I got off the phone. I found Sarah sitting on our bed crying her eyes out and reading a prayer. I felt horrible because I caused Sarah to retreat into her own world for comfort. I forgot how sensitive Sarah is and how much she understands about what is going on around her. I wish so much that I could control my anger. Sarah doesn't deserve those outbursts.

On April 6, 1997, Sarah said, "Why don't you put me in a home or dump me into the ocean." She kept repeating and repeating that for days and weeks.

During July, 1997, the deterioration continued. Sarah no longer recognized the ring of the telephone. That drove her insane. She gets all upset, flustered and cries when the telephone rings because she doesn't know where the sound is coming from. She picks up everything in sight, but never finds the phone. She can stare right at the telephone but she doesn't recognize it any longer. She doesn't recognize anything when she takes it out of the dishwasher either. She piles things all over the kitchen table and counter tops. Occasionally, she will put them in the most unlikely places and it takes me days to find whatever she has misplaced. I realize that she is trying her best, so I back off and let her do her thing. I go back and correct everything later without letting her see me do it. That makes my resentment level rise. I am constantly fixing things. Most recently, I discovered that I need to be one step ahead of her after dark because she is not able to turn the lights on in any room. If she goes to the bathroom or to the bedroom alone, I normally hear her scream or cry because she ran into something or fell. I turn appropriate lights on at sunset for safety sake. Things are constantly getting worse. Sarah loses some activity or ability every day that she never gets back.

On 8/1/97, Sarah answered what she thought was the telephone. She picked up the television remote and shouted, "Hello, hello, hello. Who is this?" She glanced over at me and saw that I was already talking on the phone. She looked at the remote as she put it on the coffee table and we both began laughing hysterically. It was yet another example of the comic defense.

The changes were more and noticeable. I was overwhelmed and resentful because I was losing control. I was not able to do anything about the progression of the identity thief. I wanted to lash out at everyone and everything. Resentment built in my mind and was taking over. I prayed and relied upon my faith to get me through this difficult period of time.

It didn't matter if it was at church, the supermarket, a department store, or beauty shop Sarah's progression was becoming more and more obvious. I reached a point that seeing couples having a good time together bothered me. I was envious of them because I no longer had that with Sarah. I missed our relationship as a couple. I was embarrassed whenever Sarah's behavior attracted attention. I struggled to adapt to my new way of life, which initially I did not like or understand.

It goes without saying that Sarah was also following a difficult path as the victim of the identity thief, especially in the early stages of her progression. As Sarah's short and long-term memories disappeared, she was granted a lack of awareness toward bliss that I did not experience.

It may seem that I have painted a negative picture of a care-partner's role. There is nothing further from the truth. I want everyone to be aware that at times, the role of a care-partner will not be glamorous. It will not be an exciting or a very rewarding existence; however, you and only you are in charge of your destiny. Remember, bitter or better is always at your disposal as you move through the care-partner milestones. It is your responsibility to keep stress within your own tolerance limits. Be proactive and do everything in your power to reduce and/or eliminate negativism. When there seems to be no light at the end of the tunnel, and this will likely occur often, sit back; take a deep, deep breath to get plenty of fresh air into your lungs. Use this quick charge technique often to get oxygen into your lungs and rejuvenate yourself. Exhale slowly and repeat and concentrate on two power-filled words, I can! The ball is in your court. You can survive as a care-partner with a minimal amount of scar tissue, but it will take faith and love, prayer, patience, desire, time, effort, and hard work. You must have a strong desire to be and stay positive in order to move successfully through the care-partner stages.

LESSONS LEARNED

• Resentment blended with anger is the second milestone in the development of a care-partner.

• Resentment can be described as unresolved anger.

• Resentment normally follows denial after involvement in a traumatic incident.

• Resentment encourages a care-partner to develop an "ain't it awful syndrome."

• Care-partners must guard against feeling a predisposition to negativism.

• Uncontrolled resentment will become counterproductive mixture.

• 'Bitter' is the easy and comfortable road that can result in stagnation and becoming 'stuck in the past'

• 'Better' means hard work, creativity and survival.

• It normally results in survival, growth, and maturity as a care-partner.

• The ten most important ten letter words that you will ever learn as a care-partner are: If it is to be, it is up to me.

Chapter 4
ALTERATION OF PERSONALITY

On 8/9/97, Sarah said, "I was scared and I did not believe the diagnosis. I went to the University of Virginia, uh Johns Hopkins University and Eastern Virginia Mili... uh, Medical School and uh nobody could say that there was anything they could do. Uh and a—they gave us some medications. None of themedications really worked—if they worked they worked for a little bit or they didn't work at all and now there's not anything and uh (unintelligible). I have a beautiful support group with my family. They're around all the time for me."

This is the most interesting and critical of all of the care-partner milestones. The personality that emerges during the alteration of personality will determine your success or failure. You will be in the super bowl of care-partnering. There are no schools for the average person drafted. Textbooks, scrimmages, practices, timeouts, and cookbooks are not available to familiarize you with the awesome responsibilities and unique challenges involved. List the signs, symptoms, and behaviors displayed by a dementia patient and I will find another who will show some, but not all of them. That is what makes your role so difficult.

I am honored to discuss this important transition that I witnessed in myself and other care-partners. I haven't found anything written about it, nor have I heard it discussed. I am of the opinion that care-partners experience a period of development and maturation during which their personality is reorganized. I called it alteration of personality to emphasize that during this third step care-partners undergo major, atypical, and strange changes. The personality is likely to change to the point that family members and friends might not recognize them any longer. This typically occurs when the new care-partner with limited experience passes to the middle stage of dementia with his/her loved one. This is the point at which I developed this new makeup. The focus of my life changed. I developed tunnel vision that permitted me to think only about the care of my wife because nothing else mattered.

This was a challenging chapter because this unique personality is the key to the survival. I took on the care-partner personality years after I developed and lived with the police personality. That combination challenged me to compare the two. There was no formal study involved in my work; rather, it involved a review my experiences, and observations in the criminal justice subculture along with those made during the years that I cared for Sarah.

This new personality develops with time and experience. I noticed that it became more visible a few years into Sarah's progression. James Wagenvoord in his book, Men – a Book for Women (1978) lists the 'Commandments of Masculinity.' These orders provide an excellent picture of the features that make up the police personality. They are right on target.

COMMANDMENTS OF MASCULINITY

He shall not cry.
He shall not display weakness.
He shall not need affection or gentleness or warmth.
He shall comfort but not desire comforting.
He shall be needed but not need.
He shall touch but not be touched.
He shall be steel not flesh.
He shall be inviolate in his manhood.
He shall stand alone.

I assert that these commandments become guidelines for police officers early in their careers. They apply to male and female officers who learn that they are not expected to show emotion because it is a perceived weakness. I call it 'image armor.' It involves burying emotions alive, which is a recipe for disaster. I did my share of overusing and abusing it. It is a second nature. It leads to a loss of sensitivity by officers, especially toward their spouses; hence, they experience high divorce rates.

Care-partners develop a personality that is similar to that of officers. Law enforcement literature documents that the police personality exists. It emerges during the first three to four years of an officer's career as a survival mode. Rookies are described as open-minded and idealistic. They exhibit a social worker type of mentality with the idea of doing good, helping others, curtailing crime, and most importantly changing the world. They exhibit a need to be in control of themselves, their emotions and the situations to which they are exposed. They are efficient, effective, and show pride. They display honesty, integrity, consistency, and leadership. They consistently set high standards for themselves as problem solvers.

Care-partners also follow the commandments of masculinity. They produce a personality that mirrors that of police officers. Here are some of the similarities that exist between the two. Care-partners start their careers open minded and idealistic with the intention of doing good for their loved ones. Their primary focus is to make the world a better place for their loved one as their life is diminished by the identity thief. They are in control of themselves and their loved ones, their emotions and the situations to which they are exposed. They exhibit pride, honesty, integrity, consistency, leadership. They set high standards for themselves. They are problem solvers while making every effort to be efficient and effective.

Ways to wear down the morale and performance of officers include increasingly demanding responsibilities, low pay, boredom, and physical and emotional stress. Combine that over time with constant work overload, lack of support and role conflict and burnout will result. Officer survival dictates the emergence of the police vs. bad guy mentality. They program themselves to trust no one outside of the law enforcement community. They do what no one else in our society wants or bothers to do, which leads to isolation from family and friends. That becomes more evident when you add shift work and the fact that you are on call 24/7 and often working long tedious hours.

The same is true for care-partners. Survival necessitates developing a care-partner vs. non-care-partner mentality. They program themselves to trust no one outside of their community, because they perceive that others do not understand or appreciate what care-partners must do daily. Care-partners do what no one else in our society wants or bothers to do. That attitude leads to isolation from family and friends.

Before too many years, the open-minded and idealistic police officer's personality grows into a cynical, super-serious, emotionally withdrawn, and strongly authoritarian officer. They are likely to become cocky and show off by their very mannerisms, and appearance. They tend to speak, and rely heavily on their badges. They gravitate toward talking insensitively, not feeling or showing emotion or trusting anyone, especially when their own emotions are involved. They believe that they are always right and do not permit themselves to admit that they can or have made a mistake. The internalizing and burying emotions alive create an unhealthy lifestyle. This culture shock eventually takes its toll. They transition through this growth, protective and survival mode which is called the 'John Wayne/Calamity Jane Syndrome.' Officers become invincible. Fortunately, only a small percentage of officers get stuck in this period. Those officers are likely to be poor performers and get into trouble.

Care-partners develop a similar personality. This can be attributed to the perception that their freedom is gone and they are under house arrest 24/7. There is no time off, compensatory time or vacation. They are not able to go or do anything alone.

They are likely to become cocky and show off by their mannerisms, and appearance that they are good and competent care-partners. They tend to speak and rely heavily about their care-partnering experiences. They gravitate toward talking insensitively, not showing emotion or trusting anyone, especially when their own emotions are involved. They believe that they are always right and they do not admit that they can or have made a mistake. The internalizing and burying alive of emotions creates an unhealthy lifestyle. They neglect their own health because they worry only about that of their loved ones. They expect excellence in their performance. They are their own worst enemy because they expect more and more of themselves as the disease progresses. They never admit that the care is going beyond their capabilities. They will never admit when they are out of their comfort zone. Here is my interpretation of the care-partner personality, which I call the 'Mighty Mouse Syndrome' with the motto – 'Here I am to save the day.' Those words translate into 'I can do it all – No help needed' for some care-partners.

The Care-partner Personality

'Mighty Mouse Syndrome = 'Here I am to save the day' = 'I can do it all – no help needed'

On duty 24/7

Under House Arrest—not able to do what you want—when you want to do it – all future plans and dreams disappear

Overwhelmed

Will not ask for help – sign of weakness/failure

Lose family and friends

Rigid

Expert at what you do

No one else can do what you can do

Isolated and lonely

Focus only on loved one – neglect own health and well-being

Enjoys researching and learning more about Alzheimer's/dementia

Very hard on oneself – OWN WORST ENEMY—expecting complete and total excellence

The longer that you are a care-partner, the more difficult it will be to 'let go' of that responsibility following the death of loved one. This is especially true in the case of spouses.

Care-partners develop tunnel vision when it comes to their loved ones. That puts them at a disadvantage because they become narrow minded. They attend support groups but they do not always follow through on the advice and suggestions offered. They disregard the information received or they become obsessed with it. There does not appear to be any middle road for some care-partners. They believe that no other human being is capable of taking care of their loved one in the same special, caring, loving, and professional way that they have been accustomed to doing. Thus, care-partners shy away from any type of respite. Some can't even trust their loved ones in the hands of professionals at an adult day center or other type of facility. They rationalize their lack of trust by blaming the refusal on their loved ones.

The 'Mighty Mouse Syndrome' can become counterproductive when it is overused and abused. It clouds your ability to think clearly about your loved ones care. Unfortunately, many care-partners are programmed to go it alone. This should be avoided at all costs. Care-partners must be enlightened to prevent this from becoming a reality. Unfortunately, it normally takes a tragedy, crisis or health issue to get the attention of a care-partner who is not willing to implement necessary changes.

This is a perfect time for me to show you some of Sarah's writings and daily activities as further proof of the difficulties she was experiencing as my personality was changing. This should give you a better appreciation of Sarah's abilities during the middle to the latter part of the year 1977. Her Alzheimer's moved slowly and deliberately, as it stole bits and pieces of her brain daily. (Refer to illustrations at center of book.)

Sarah was always very affectionate and loved to call me 'snuggle-bunny.' She got more confused during the middle stage. She signed her cards as 'SB' or 'Snuggle Bunny.' She switched pet names because she was 'sweet pea.' Multi-tasking was impossible at this point.

Mini-Incidents occurring August – November 1997

On 8/19/97, Sarah and I were asleep. At 2:00 am, she picked at me, which woke me up. I tried to ignore her, but she kept picking and picking. I was getting anxious and frustrated. I sat up and asked her what she was doing. She said, "Do you see them? There are snakes and squiggles are all over you. They are falling down in the air – look at them they are all over you." I did not see a thing. She continued to pick and pick. She tried to catch whatever she saw in mid-air. I wanted to get back to sleep, but Sarah was not interested in sleep until she got rid of those things that were all over my body. I remained calm with the hope that she would fall back to sleep. It was another of those nights that come out of nowhere.

I distracted Sarah by taking her to the bathroom and giving her something to drink. I put her back into the bed after fifteen minutes of talking and walking. That was enough of a distraction. Sarah forgot about the snakes and the squiggles and we were both able to get back to sleep.

On 8/30/97, Sarah walked our dog in the dog patch at our condominium. This grassy area was at the edge of Linkhorn Bay. I watched Sarah and Skipper from the deck of our condo. I heard a splash and saw that Skipper had jumped into the bay to catch a duck. I panicked because Sarah was walking onto the rocks and was about to go into the water to help Skipper. Fortunately, a neighbor was walking past her at the time and stopped her. I called to the neighbor and asked her to stay with Sarah until I could get there from the second floor. By the time I arrived at the dog patch, Sarah was happily talking to our neighbor as Skipper made his way out of the water. From that point on, I had to be with Sarah whenever she walked Skipper. I must be at her side whenever she walks the dog, but I dare not tell her why because that will upset her. She is already bothered by the fact that I have to do so much for and with her now. I will make up a lame excuse about needing exercise and wanting to keep her safe and away from all the muggers and rapists because she is so beautiful.

On 11/10/97, I realized that Sarah resents me for helping her to do anything that she is not able to do any longer. She is taking her frustrations out on me which stinks. No one understands or cares about what I am going through. It is so deceiving because of her age. No one, including myself wants to believe that she has Alzheimer's disease. I wish I could get into her head and see what she is going through and feel what she is feeling. I bet that would put me in a better position to help her.

On 11/20/97, Sarah watered the same plants 3 or 4 times. She is driving me crazy, because it is impossible to correct or stop her from doing things. If she gets something into her mind there is no changing that. The plants are overflowing on the floor and she doesn't notice it. She keeps watering and watering. If I ask her to stop and tell her why, she gets angry and cries. Then she'll spend hours alone in her room in some type of a trance. I feel sorry for her, but she is getting impossible to deal with.

Mini-Incidents during 1998

On 4/8/98, I left Sarah alone in the morning to go to an Alzheimer's meeting. I called frequently to check on her, but the phone was busy. I arrived home 4 hours later. Sarah was very upset; in fact, she was a basket case. She was not able to hang the telephone up. She ran the dishwasher twice. She made four slices of toast, but only wanted two. That really confused her. She forgot how to spread the peanut butter on her toast. It was definitely not safe to leave her home alone even for a few hours.

On 4/21/98, we moved to Chesterfield, Virginia to be closer to our children and grandchildren. I thought that it was a good move because I should be able to get much needed help and support.

Sarah continues to be bothered by daily and severe headaches. She also has acute gastro-intestinal pain and discomfort. There is no middle of the road for her because it is either diaherra or constipation. She has unexplained fainting spells or episodes of syncope. Blood work and medical procedures such as EKGs, MRIs, Cat Scans, wearing of a heart monitor have not determined the source of these spells. It is a mystery that has continued throughout the progression of the identity thief.

Mini-Incidents continue through 1999

On 3/5/99, Sarah said, "I am such a burden. You have to do everything."

On 10/21/99, Sarah was diagnosed with adult bacteria acne, which causes her to pick at her forehead, nose and chin until they bleed. The picking has become more and more obvious and annoying to those around her, including myself. The doctor provided ointments for daily use, but Sarah would not use them. It was a chore to get Sarah to agree to let me to put the meds on her to prevent infection. It was exhausting convincing her that she needed them. Once I put them on her she would pick again and wipe them off. It was a never ending and frustrating battle.

Things never seem to get better. More and more work gets dumped on me. To add to this, Sarah developed an aversion to any restrictive clothing around her waist. Pants with elastic were a no-no. Jeans or any type of pants aggravated her. I thought ahead and outside of the box. I only put loose fitting dresses on her. The same applied at bedtime. I had to use loose nightgowns and avoid pajamas with an elastic waistband. I definitely had to change because Sarah was no longer capable of changing.

On 10/29/99, Sarah, "I think I'm going to die. I am in the process of dying. I just finished saying a few prayers. I'm not ready to go just yet, but I don't know what's wrong. Nothing feels right. Nothing is working. Oh, please help me. I think I am dying." She was in bed at the time.

On 11/7/99 Sarah said, "Will you help me? I don't know what to do with these." She was holding an armful of clothes. Later, she put a dirty dish in the freezer and then into the refrigerator. She didn't recognize the dishwasher. Watching those behaviors drives me crazy. Sarah tried hard to help me, but it was less of a problem if she did nothing because she put things in the strangest places. I find her mistakes and correct them before they create a problem. My being a neat freak made this even more stressful.

On 11/28/99, I admit that I miss not being able to communicate with Sarah. I can't share anything because she doesn't understand me. I have no one to share my innermost thoughts, feelings and emotions with. That is disturbing. Sarah has always been there and acted as my sounding board. I felt safe talking to or telling her anything. Now, whenever she talks it's as if she is speaking in a foreign language. I feel isolated and alone. She doesn't recognize her children by name. She refers to them as him or her. Holidays do not have the same meaning any more. I dread birthdays, anniversaries, Christmas, Thanksgiving. I do not need them because Sarah could care less.

On 12/5/99, I found that sleeping is a problem for the both of us. Sarah is restless, anxious and up and down throughout the night. She wants to wander throughout the house. She mumbles constantly and sees things that aren't there. I have no idea what she wants or where she is going, but I am convinced that she is on some type of a mission. Something motivates her, although I will probably never know or understand what it is. It is not unusual for her to get up at 4:00 am and get dressed. She wants to go somewhere, but she is not able to express it. She is in and out of the bathroom throughout the night. I usually get up and wander with her to make sure that she does not hurt herself or get into trouble. I have no idea how long this will go on, but I am wearing out without adequate sleep. I will ask the doctor for suggestions about her nighttime wandering.

On 12/30/99, Sarah appeared like she was in a trance this morning when she said, "Father Bill (her uncle) made me this way. I am angry at him. Why did he do this to me? I never did anything to him." All of a sudden, she snapped out of it and was a different person for the remainder of the day.

Sarah continues to have difficulty getting into the car. She does not recognize the door or door handle. I have to physically open the door and show her how to sit down; otherwise, she stands there and stares, as I repeat instructions for her. It is not unusual for her to get into a stranger's vehicle, even if there is someone is sitting in it. I have to hold her hand in a parking lot to make sure that she does not get into the wrong car or walk into traffic. She has no sense of danger. Everything is getting worse.

Sarah started something new. She puts her used toilet paper into the waist paper basket rather than the toilet. I hate it because I have not been able to find a way to stop her from doing that without causing a major incident. She has a mental block about doing it any other way, so I am forced to follow behind her and discretely clean up.

Every day she puts her shoes on the wrong feet. When I change them, she insists that they are on the right feet. She argues about everything, especially if I correct or help her. I avoid arguing at all costs but that is not the easiest thing to do. Sarah doesn't make anything easy for me. My job is tough enough without her constantly wanting to argue. She doesn't understand or appreciate that I am her friend and I am trying to help. I am frustrated and exhausted.

Sarah loves to fold laundry; however, she puts all of her clothes into my dresser drawers, instead of her own. It is frustrating to have to follow behind her, without her knowledge, and rearrange the drawers.

She constantly puts frozen foods into the vegetable bins instead of the freezer. I try to move them quickly into the freezer without Sarah seeing me, but that is not always an easy task.

Sarah is obsessed with shaving her legs with a real razor. She misses hair in patches and cuts her legs like crazy. She bleeds all over the place. It takes me a while to stop the bleeding and get her cleaned up. I purchased a portable electric shaver that I now use to shave her legs and underarms. Once again, I have another chore. I am more and more overwhelmed and over-loaded. It doesn't seem fair.

Dressing is frustrating. She gets confused and comes out of the bedroom with several layers or no clothes on. It is not unusual for her to wear 2 bras, 2 blouses, or 2 pair of underwear. She came out dressed for bed one evening wearing clean jeans, a bra, one slipper and one sock. I couldn't help laughing out loud as Sarah said, "Something is wrong." She continued, "I thought that would give you a good laugh." It is so frustrating. I lay Sarah's clothes out on the bed every morning and evening, but she ignores those and finds something different in the closet or dresser.

I must find the key to her letting me help to get her dressed. There must be a secret. I just haven't found it yet. Yes, this adds another responsibility, but hopefully when I find the secret Sarah will be much more relaxed and that will make this easier.

Sarah has difficulty swallowing pills. She is falling a lot. She complains constantly about headaches and a pain in her abdomen and/or stomach, but the doctors find nothing wrong. I am tired of taking her to the doctors for nothing. I'm wondering if she is a hypochondriac. She scratches and picks at her face and forehead. She stays up all night long. She doesn't seem to need or enjoy sleeping.

On 1/12/00, Sarah said, "I think I am going to die." I asked her if anything hurt her and she said, "Everything, nothing is right, I'm dying."

On 6/1/00, Sarah began to take Exelon. Perhaps, this will be just what she needs so that we can both get some relief. Later that day she said, "I can't talk."

On 6/5/00, Sarah woke up at 5:00 am. She was tossing and turning. She woke me up, but I tried not to let her know that I was awake. I wanted her to go back to sleep. She started rubbing my back and said repeatedly, 'I love you.' She kept asking, 'What are we going to do?' I finally had to get out of bed. That was the end of my sleep for that day.

It was early in the morning and my stress level was already on the way up.

On 6/28/00, Sarah appeared to be in a trance today. All she could say was yes or no.

On 7/6/00, Sarah was not able to find me in the house even though I was running the vacuum full-blast. She was upset and disoriented. She spoke rapidly and in a word salad. I had no idea what she was trying to say. I don't know if it was the noise of the vacuum that scared her or something else. I gave her a big hug. That calmed her down at least for the moment. I stopped using the vacuum in case the noise bothered her.

On 7/11/00, we reached a major milestone. Sarah's doctor noted Sarah's decline and my stress. She suggested that Sarah attend an adult day center. To encourage her participation, the doctor wrote specific instructions on a prescription form.

I thought that Sarah was too young to attend. Fortunately, after conversations with my friends at the Alzheimer's Association, I realized that it was the correct thing to do. I knew down deep that I had to do something that would benefit the both of us. I needed to get away from Sarah and she needed to get away from me. I enrolled Sarah in an adult day center two days a week.

On 7/25/00, I found a small adult day center called, Senior Options II. That was perfect for our needs. I eventually moved her up to five days a week. It was break for the both of us and a relief for me. I dropped Sarah off at 8:00am and picked her up at 4:00pm. I was in seventh heaven. I could do anything that I wanted during the day—sleep, background investigations, cleaning, laundry, volunteer work, or shopping. What a tremendous resource that I would never have thought was available.

On 7/30/00, Sarah got up at 4:00 am and dressed for work. Sarah has been retired for seven years and she still occasionally thinks that she must go to work.

She had no idea what I was talking about when I told her that she was retired. I had to be creative and tell her that it was a Saturday or Sunday or a vacation day. I said whatever I had to say to avoid upsetting Sarah.

On 8/15/00, Sarah kept repeating, "I'm scared. I think I'm dying. I don't know what's happening to me."

On 8/28/00, Sarah came out of the bathroom with all of her toilet articles in a bag and said, "I want to go home." She was confused and in a trance. It took a lot of tender loving care to distract her and help her to relax.

On 9/13/00, Sarah couldn't relax. Her anxiety was out of control. She wanted to do something, but she didn't know what. She rejected all of my suggestions. Sarah finally said, "I'm bored. I don't know what I can do."

At about 8:00 pm that evening, I asked Sarah if she would draw and put the current time on a clock. She worked on it for quite a while. I gave her a little space and did something else so that I would not distract her. I was shocked when I saw the results. It was a sure sign that the dementia was there and at work. Refer to illustrations in the center of this book to see Sarah's clock drawing.

On 9/30/00, Sarah told me that she wanted to go to the bathroom. She had no idea where the bathroom was in our house. Toileting is more and more of a problem. Sarah cannot clean herself properly, which is a sanitary issue. I have always feared incontinence and it is approaching quickly. That could very well end my career as a care-partner. I don't know how I am going to handle this crisis. That thought kept me up nights.

On 11/26/00, Sarah needed the bathroom, but she could not find it in the house. She didn't recognize it when she saw it. This is true for so many things.

On 12/3/00, everything is getting worse. Sarah can't find the bathroom or bedroom, kitchen, tissues or anything else in the house. She woke up from a powernap at 4:45pm crying and said, "I'm afraid of them – It's different – I want to go home."

On 12/26/00, I thought about Christmas day. This holiday season has always been special for Sarah, but it meant nothing to her this year. She had no interest in decorating, buying gifts or celebrating. She was in her own world, but I figured I would carry on the tradition for her. I put on a show for Sarah's benefit. We talked a lot and bonded together during this holiday. We also cried at the fact that Sarah had lost so much. Those were special moments. She appeared more aware than usual that the Alzheimer's had taken so much from her. I prayed for help, extra strength and patience.

On 1/7/01, I heard Sarah walking in the bedroom closet at 4:00 am. She was in a trance and mumbling in word salad. She blurted out, "I can't find anyone." I eventually eased her back into bed after a few hugs and sweet talk.

On 1/9/01, Sarah was quiet and content watching television. She became very anxious. It took time and patience to calm her down because she couldn't tell why she was so upset. She finally told me that they were talking about her on the television program. They were talking about putting her someplace. She could only recall bits of what was said. I reassured her that they were not talking about her and she was safe with me. I turned the program off and calmed her with a lot of TLC.

Sarah & Bob with (l – r) Sean, Tom, Bobby & Kathy in 1976

Sarah & Bob at show time

8/19/97

②

Buu

Beach BUP

with

BU

Beach BUB

a step

Closer

to AV.

Ab minor

Sarah

RoBn

RoIN

RoBIN

RobIN

SARAH'S PRINTING
PM 9/9/97

ARKANS

ARKA ARKSAS

ARKASI

Happy Father's Day
I Love you so much
Hope I and and Hope
I don't get an worse
you are my "Best"
Friend

8/19/97
Tandums ①
Dinner
Tandums

Down were
Bardie
lives
Her m and
& Medical asselants
PoB is at the
with

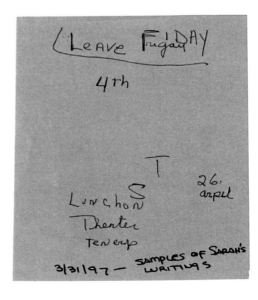

(Leave Friday
4th

T
S   26.
Lunchon   arpil
Theater
Ten erp
3/31/97 —   SAMPLES OF SARAH'S
            WRITINGS

Happy Valentine's Day

From yours Snugge Bunny
T

I love you.

THis Card
Thank says it all
for Being my
SURPORT

I ASKED SARAH
TO DRAW A
CLOCK
8^{00} pm 9/13/00
under relaxed
conditions

Sarah in assisted living – July 2003

Sarah on Christmas day – 2003

Sarah with Bob as Santa, Kathy, Holly, Kourtney & Sommer

Sarah's birthday – 2/24/04

Sarah with daughter Kathy and granddaughters, Kourtney, Sommer & Holly in Courtyard at Lucy Corr Village on 6/25/05

Jackie (my sister) with Sarah in Courtyard at Lucy Corr Village

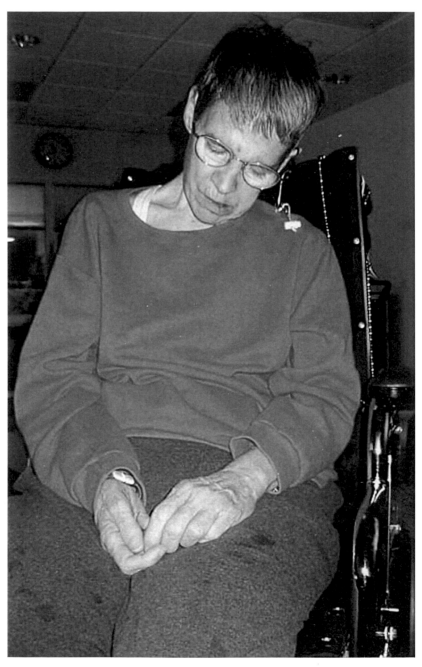

Sarah experiencing episode of syncope on 7/7/06

Sarah – just one week later- on 7/13/06

The Schaefer Family pays tribute to Sarah by performing a Christmas Concert for residents in the Clover Hill Neighborhood – Christmas 2007

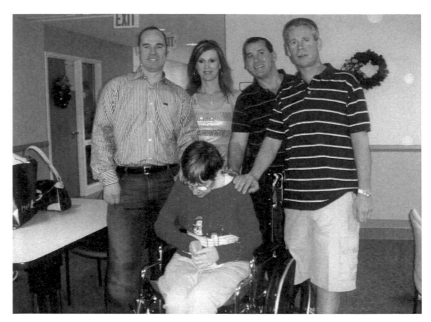

Sean, Kathy, Bobby & Tom with their Mother - Christmas 2007

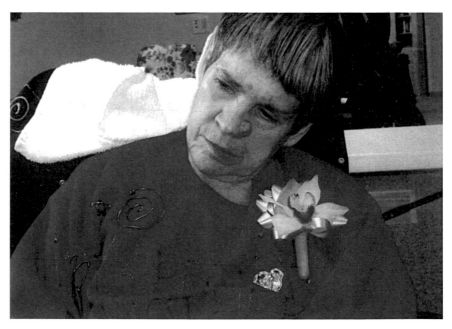

Sarah on Mother's Day – May 11, 2008

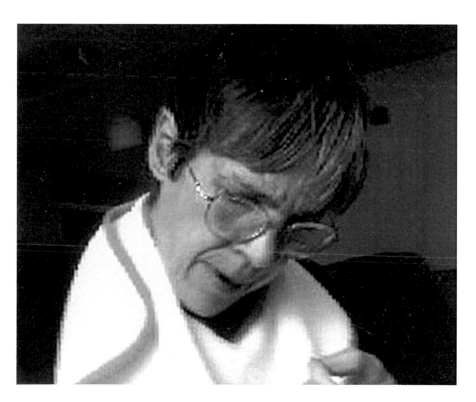

Sarah on 10/6/08 (Episode of syncope)

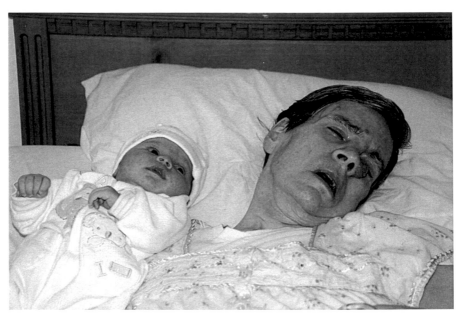

**Sarah meets her 11th grandchild Mikayla—On 11/13/08—
Three weeks before she died.**

On 1/18/01, I tucked Sarah into bed at 8:00 pm. As I was leaving she said, "I hope that I don't do anything bad tonight." My heart went out to her. With all of her problems, she still worries about me. It amazed me that she remembered that she had caused a problem several nights ago. At times, her short term memory flickers on and off like a loose light bulb.

On 1/23/01, I noticed that Sarah gets up in the middle of the night to wander around the house. She paces back and forth. I have been sleeping on the couch because she is so restless in the bed. She always finds her way out of the bedroom. That wakes me automatically. Sarah is in a trance when she wanders during the night. I get exasperated because I cannot communicate with or get into her world. I want to help, but there is no penetrating that shell. I have been exhausted lately.

On 2/4/01, Sarah keeps asking the same questions over and over again. I get tired of being nice. I want to scream, but that makes things worse. She asks, "Can I have some money? Is there any food? Are we going to church today? Who is coming for dinner tonight?" I know that she doesn't realize that she is asking the questions repeatedly, but when you are in the middle of it, that doesn't help much.

On 2/6/01, I lost my temper and yelled at Sarah because she paced all night long. I felt bad yelling. Yelling causes her to fall apart, but it is difficult to think clearly when you are so exhausted.

On 2/19/01, I observed that Sarah was unusually anxious. She put her coat on and kept saying that she wanted to go home. I was so tired and frustrated that I opened the door and let her go out by herself to walk in the driveway. What a mistake. I took my eyes off her for two minutes and she was gone. Panic set in because I couldn't find her. I checked ours and the neighbor's yards with no luck. I wrestled with calling the police, but decided to wait and search for her by car. I found Sarah walking at a fast pace, about three blocks from our house. She was relieved that I found her because she had no idea where she was going or what she was doing. I must get over my reluctance to call the police immediately when Sarah wanders away. It might be the difference between life and death.

On 2/25/01, Sarah repeatedly asked me how old she was yesterday. I answered her as calmly as I could by saying, "You were 60 yesterday. Isn't that great?" Sarah said, "Oh no, I feel like I am five today."

On 2/27/01, Sarah started something new. Instead of putting her used toilet paper into the waste-paper basket as she had previously done, she was putting it in the pockets of her jeans, pants or jacket. It was such a sensitive issue because Sarah thought that she was doing the right thing. She became angry with me if she saw me remove it from her pockets. I had to be clever and often wait until the end of the day to empty her pockets. I considered it to be a health issue, so I always tried to distract her during the day, so that I could clean her pockets out. Sometimes I was able to do it like a magician, while other times, I got her upset and agitated. I'm trying my best, but it is not easy. There is no right or wrong answer to many of these situations. It's thinking outside the box to invent something that will work for you and your loved one.

On 3/1/01, something new has surfaced again. Sarah tries to go to the bathroom by herself, but is unable to get herself dressed again. She gets frustrated because she has no idea what she is doing wrong. When I attempt to help her, she gets agitated and lashes out. She says that I do not know what I am doing. Her resistance to my helping her is getting worse. I guess that she is that embarrassed that she is not able to help herself.

On 3/14/01, Sarah began to have trouble swallowing her pills. She holds them in her mouth. It does not matter how much water she swallows, she hides the pills somewhere in her mouth or under her tongue. She has never had a problem taking anything up to this point. Here we go with something new that I have to overcome.

On 3/15/01, I was proactive and innovative. I picked up a pill crusher at the pharmacy. I crushed Sarah's pills and put them in pudding, apple sauce or ice cream. That solved the medication problems. I consulted our pharmacist to make sure that this could be done without any problem.

On 3/31/01, Sarah used a public restroom on our trip back from Florida. She was so embarrassed that a little girl had to lead her out because she was not able to find the exit door. I must be at Sarah's side whenever she uses the restroom on trips. I have dreaded this, but it is here to stay and I will deal with it with a smile.

On 4/12/01, Sarah is sticking to me like glue. We do everything together. She even follows me into the bathroom. It is impossible for me to get out of her sight 24/7 and if I ever take my eyes off her for even 30 seconds, she is gone. It happens that quickly. My only relief comes when Sarah is at the adult day center. I never thought that I would say this, but I would never have made it this far without that as a safety valve.

On 4/14/01, Sarah has been doing well at Senior Options II. We were notified that they will be closing due to financial problems. Thank God for the Alzheimer's Association. With their lists, I located another adult day center at Lucy Corr Village. They have a vacancy and Sarah will attend five days a week.

On 5/6/01, Sarah walked into the bathroom at 2:00 am. She thought that I had called her from there. She went back into the bathroom again at 3:00 am because it was time to get ready for church. I put her back into her bed both times without much of a problem; however, at 5:00 am, she found me sleeping on the couch in the den. She was anxious and started pacing for the rest of the night and day.

On 5/9/01, Sarah was very anxious. She wandered around the house the entire night. She was in some kind of a trance or in her own world. She heard me talking, but was not able to respond.

On 5/14/01, Sarah kept repeating, "I don't want to leave here. I really like it here." I reassured her that I would not put her into any type of a facility. She sensed that I was frustrated, overloaded and wearing out. She is paranoid that I do not want to take care of her any more. She does not believe it when I tell her that my plan has always been to keep her at home for the duration of her illness.

On 5/29/01, I noticed that Sarah wanders every night. She does not need much, if any, sleep. She constantly mumbles, "I'm sorry or I'm scared," as she wanders.

On 6/27/01, Sarah started taking razadyne. I am not asking for a miracle. I just hope that this will help her sleeping, dressing, bathing, and talking.

On 6/30/01, Sarah came to me while I was waxing the car in the garage. I had left her in the bedroom because she insisted on dressing herself. I laid her clothes out on the bed. I gave her some space. I looked up and Sarah was standing behind me. She was naked and carrying her slacks in her hand because she could not remember how to put them on. I rushed her back into the house. As we were walking toward the bedroom, I saw that she dropped her underwear on the floor of the den and her shoes in the hallway. She told me that she was trying to dress for church, even though it was not Sunday. Obviously, she was not able to dress herself.

LESSONS LEARNED

- Care-partners are drafted rather than volunteering.

- 'Alteration of Personality,' the third milestone in the development of a care-partner, which results in the development of a unique personality.

- There are no care-partner schools, rulebooks, cookbooks or scrimmages to prepare that important and stressful role.

- Care-partners think for two people and wear twenty-one separate hats.

- Wearing the Alzheimer's detective's hat will assist you to think outside the box.

- Care-partners develop the 'Mighty Mouse Syndrome' which is very similar to the John Wayne/Calamity Jane Syndrome in police officers.

- Image armor helps to prevent care-partners from overburdening or overusing their emotions.

- Care-partners, family members and friends should be aware of and monitor the alteration of personality milestone.

- A healthy care-partner seeks help.

Chapter 5
FRENZY

On 3/2/03, Sarah said, "Please don't do this to me. I love you so much."

The next developmental stage is called frenzy. Choice of that word shows the desperation that could develop in this timeframe. This is where the rubber meets the road. It could have easily been called mental derangement, madness, mania, excitement, wildness, or hysteria. Those words all reinforce how critical this milestone can be.

Frenzy will come about during the middle stage of the progression or possibly sooner for some. It surfaces during extended periods of fatigue or when you feel that you are at the end of your rope. Serious doubts arise about the desire, and ability to continue. The care of your loved will dominate your life. You may seriously consider giving up and throwing in the towel. It can be the longest and most demanding leg of your journey through Alzheimer's. You are likely to ignore health problems, which could amount to an unconscious death wish. This will occur at the same time that your new personality is calling the shots. You will feel lost and likely on the path to destruction; however, the good news is that this does not have to be the case. You have choices.

It is during this backdrop that crazy visions about outside help torment you. It doesn't matter if it is in-home, an adult day center, assisted living facility, or a skilled nursing facility. It is clear that you will not need or want help. It can be a source of torment because your new personality will constantly demand that you go it alone. Asking for help is definitely perceived to be a sign of weakness or failure.

I was not only plagued by the agony of Sarah's care, but also difficult and unexplained behaviors that occurred more and more frequently. They became increasingly more burdensome to deal with and resolve. I was drained and losing my patience more often. I was haunted by the reality that I might be forced to go outside the home for care. The 'Mighty Mouse Syndrome' urged me to push forward and ignore thoughts of outside help. It kept telling me that I was doing an excellent job of caring for Sarah. I was a macho police officer and FBI agent. I didn't need outside help.

Asking for help would show everyone that I was human. Thinking that continued to be in conflict with my motto of, 'Here I am to save the day.' It took all of my remaining psyche, strength and energy to ignore those words that were such a large part of me. I have learned that it is best to reach out for help early; however, but if you fail to do that like I did, there is still hope. You have the opportunity to do a u-turn. It is never too late to change. I decided to reach before it was too late. Never attempt to do it alone. That will be a losing battle. Learn from my mistakes. Reaching out was a difficult truth. I had to go against the personality that was controlling me, but my desire to survive helped me to accomplish that.

Care-partners must protect and preserve their health and well-being. That doesn't come naturally with your makeup. I ignored many of the early warning signs when I was in this stage. I forgot that if something happened to me no one would be there to take care of Sarah. That thought was a powerful motivator.

I learned the hard way. I finally took advantage of my daughter's offer to take Sarah several hours a day so that I could work part-time. That gave me a temporary diversion and respite from responsibilities because I trusted my daughter. I did that until Sarah's anxiety level increased to the point that she was too difficult to handle. She was paranoid that I was going to abandon her. She spent all her time looking for me or asking Kathy when I was going to return. She wanted to leave Kathy's home constantly to search for me.

The breaks from my duties were great. It eased some of the pain that I was experiencing. It reinforced the fact that I should send Sarah to an adult day center as a continuing source of respite. The day center was not Sarah's favorite activity, but she didn't offer much resistance to it. That made it bearable for us both. Between the adult day center and Kathy, I kept Sarah at home for an additional five years.

The frenzy stage heightened during the middle stage of Sarah's Alzheimer's. With all of the anxiety, paranoia, mini-incidents and difficult and unusual behaviors appearing more regularly, I was losing my mind. Strange, bizarre and evil, gloomy thoughts cluttered my mind all day and night. I could not stop them. They wore me out. That was not good because I took my frustrations out on Sarah. I was short, abrupt and angry all the time. I didn't sleep or eat well. Whenever I did fall asleep, it was a restless sleep for minutes at a time full of bad dreams, nightmares or other interruptions. Feelings of isolation and loneliness overpowered me. I didn't think clearly because of the crazy ideas swirling in my head. They were so bizarre that I did not share them with anyone. I feared that someone would think that I was insane and report me to Social Services or the police. I was on the verge of a nervous breakdown and I didn't have any idea what I should do. Here are examples of those disturbing thoughts:

I will divorce Sarah as soon as I can so that I will not be financially responsible for her in the future. We can live together common law, but she will be financially responsible for herself.

Where did Sarah go? I am living with a perfect stranger and I do not like it. I have to find a way out of this before I go crazy.

I made a promise that I would never put Sarah into any long-term care facility. I would kill myself before breaking my promise.

Will Sarah die before I do so that I can live a normal life and enjoy my retirement that I worked so hard for these last 35 years?

Sometimes, as a spouse, I get fed up with my role as a care-partner. I want to abandon her and ignore the wedding vows – "for better or worse."

I do it all—cooking, cleaning, laundry, grocery shopping and anything else that needs to be done. How long will I have to do this? I do not see an end in sight. This is not fair. I cannot do it any longer. I want out. I must find a way to escape from this life.

How can Sarah be so stupid? She cannot do anything. I hate her and the fact that I have to take care of her.

I can't stand the repetition, pacing, rocking back and forth, following and hovering. Every time that I turn around Sarah is behind me. There is no privacy anymore.

Sometimes I feel like I want to lie down and die. I do not have the strength to continue this.

I want to take Sarah out into the woods or to a shopping mall or some remote location and leave her there. I can't face another day as her care-partner.

My patience is non-existent with Sarah. I'm afraid that I'm going to lose my temper and abuse her in some way. A little push here or there —who would know as long as I didn't leave any marks or bruises?

Why do I have to take care of Sarah alone? Where is everyone else? Why am I being punished?

Everyone thinks that I am a loving and wonderful care-partner. How would they react if they knew about these awful thoughts that I having every day and night?

This list could go on for pages. I know that I hit home with many care-partners. You might not want to admit it, but you have had some or several of these scary and dark thoughts. They appear early, but increase in intensity significantly throughout the progression of the identity thief. They tend to stand out more during this frenzy period.

This is where the rubber meets the road. This line of thinking is a normal reaction to an abnormal situation. That makes it okay. However, that assumes that you don't take any steps to carry them out. Talk to someone as they appear. This can be done through a support group or with a close friend who has walked the walk. Or you may consult a member of the clergy or a mental health professional. The point is that you need to talk about these intrusive thoughts with someone in a non-threatening environment. That will validate your emotions. It will also help to reduce your stress. The source of the debriefing isn't as important as freeing yourself of the emotional baggage. If you do not debrief then you use up your valuable energy supply continuing to fight and repress these thoughts. That could easily lead to health and mental problems to make you unfit to continue in your efforts. Keeping a daily journal or recordings is another possible way to debrief.

Severe and unrelenting stress can weaken and destroy. Take appropriate steps to avoid those stressors that tend to get the best of you. Negative stress is cumulative and will overwhelm you, if you are not prepared. This is a critical period because you are already in a weakened state. You can be more susceptible to temptations that you might never otherwise consider. I am talking about the use of self-medications and even the possibility of suicide as viable options. Both of these and my choice of a reaching out to a mental health professional will be discussed in a later chapter.

Our lives are filled with decisions. I cannot imagine how many the average human makes every day. I earned a college education, an honorable discharge from the US Navy, became a state trooper, FBI agent, married and had children, just to mention a few. At the time, they required a lot of thought and planning and resulted in a normal amount of stress. I can say without reservation that no other decision has been as difficult to make, or has had such an impact upon my life, as those forced on me by Alzheimer's. The worst involved putting Sarah into the hands of perfect strangers in a facility. How could I possibly do that and live with myself? I am not embarrassed to admit that for weeks before and after I made that decision, I cried day and night. I was frightened and alone because nothing like that had ever happened before. I let those dark and scary thoughts get to me because I did not want to break my promise to Sarah.

I struggled to continue my commitment to Sarah and our wedding vows. I made sure that I attended support groups on a regular basis. I convinced myself that I would be able to keep Sarah at home for the duration of her illness even though her care was progressing beyond my capabilities. My confidence was shaken when I saw how much Sarah had deteriorated since her surgery. I knew that I couldn't stay up day and night to follow and protect her. I searched for an assisted living facility. My focus centered on a small facility rather than a nursing home. I thought that the smaller setting would be less traumatic for Sarah.

I visited and toured nursing homes in the Richmond area just in case an unforeseen emergency occurred in the future. I was surprised to find that there was a waiting list for most facilities with an Alzheimer's unit. I was still convinced that I would never put Sarah into a long-term care facility; however, I did put her name on several waiting lists.

The reality that Sarah was not going to ever return to the level that she was at before her surgery became evident. Incontinence was becoming an everyday, rather than an occasional problem. I was losing more control of my thoughts, feelings and emotions. My kids and friends urged me to do something before it was too late.

I revisited the ten bed assisted living facility in Hanover County that I had planned on a year earlier. I convinced myself that assisted living would better than a nursing home. I updated Sarah's paperwork and within a week, she was a resident. It was a pleasant country setting. It was not plush by any stretch, but it was clean and the level of care seemed to be more than adequate. I cried all the way home. Fortunately, Tom and Sean came out with me to drop off their mom, and Sean drove me home.

In the weeks that followed, I was lonely, depressed, embarrassed and guilty primarily because I had broken my promise. I was a failure. The only saving factor was that Sarah didn't seem to have been very affected by her move. She knew that she was not at home, but she did not outwardly react to that. That was a plus because it made the transition easier for the both of us. I made a new promise that I would visit Sarah every day. I hoped that that would overcome the guilt that I was experiencing.

I was active and visible in the daily workings of the facility. After a year there, the administrator told me that Sarah's care had progressed beyond their capabilities and regulations governing their operations. In reality, she wanted to get rid of Sarah because by doing so she could also get rid of me. I was a thorn in her side. I saw that personal care had begun to deteriorate. I was not shy about bringing problems to the attention of the administrator. She did not appreciate my interference. Unfortunately, correcting the problems that I noted required money and she did not spend money, unless it was absolutely essential. I made it clear that I would report deficiencies to the appropriate authorities if they were not corrected. Sarah was being punished unnecessarily for something that I did. Within a couple of weeks of notice to leave, I transferred Sarah to the Clover Hill Neighborhood at Lucy Corr Village.

The mini-incidents and Sarah's condition continued to deteriorate during her stay at Clover Hill. The following events will update and help you to visualize the feelings and emotions generated by the both of us. They will also establish a timeline for Sarah's progression before and during this interval of frenzy.

2001 through 2003

On 7/3/01, Sarah was not able get out of bed. Her entire body shook. She had difficulty breathing. I rushed her to the emergency room. Blood work, an EKG and chest x-rays failed to determine that anything wrong with her. We were at a loss as we returned home worrying about this happening again.

On 8/2/01, Sarah wandered out of the bedroom at 3:00 am. I was asleep on the couch. She woke me and said, "Thank God you are here. I was so scared."

On 8/16/01, Sarah said, "Please don't put me anyplace." I'm not sure what precipitated that comment. Sarah is much more alert than I give her credit for. She knows that I am wearing out and suspects that I have been thinking about long-term care for her. No one in this world knows what I feel like right now. It is horrible.

On 9/3/01, Sarah was quiet, sad and depressed. She was deep in thought, but blurted out, "I don't do some things right."

On 10/3/01, I see that accidents are happening more often when Sarah uses the bathroom. She went to the bathroom during the night. I was exhausted and passed out on the couch. I didn't hear her get up, which was unusual. The next morning when I took Sarah to the bathroom, I noticed that she had mistaken the tub for the toilet. I was angry, but I realized that she was trying. I could not be angry because she was disoriented and confused. It was not her fault. I regrouped, cleaned the tub without Sarah knowing what had happened and acted as if nothing had happened. I am taking baby steps to keep from getting angry and losing my temper.

On 10/24/01, Sarah had a panic attack in the middle of the night. I heard her yelling. When I opened the door, she screamed, "Please don't hurt me." It took me a long time to calm her down. After that, neither of us was able to get back to sleep. I stayed with her and she spent the rest of the night mumbling about her father.

On 10/26/01, I made a mistake. I left Sarah in the car by herself, while I ran into a store for a quick errand. I returned and drove away from the curb. All of a sudden, the passenger door flew open and Sarah started to fall out. I reached over and grabbed her jacket to prevent her falling on the road. It was a good thing that there were no other cars in front or behind us. Sarah tried to follow me, but I came back too soon. She took her seat belt off and opened the door, but by the time that she had done that I was back and driving away.

On 12/15/01, Sarah stuck to me like glue. It broke my heart because she keeps asking if I am going to continue to take care of her. She follows that by telling me how much she loves me. She is smart. She senses what is going on in my mind, even with her Alzheimer's. It hurts to lie to her. I cannot tell her what I am planning. It not fair that we should have to go through this. Every time that I am ready to place her in a nursing home she does something that tears me up and I doubt my own judgment.

On 1/4/02, Sarah was not able to hold her head up; consequently, she can't focus on anyone or anything. It is the same way walking, standing or sitting. If I lift her head it bothers her. The doctors can't explain it other than saying that it is the progression.

On 1/16/02, Sarah went into the bathroom. By the time I realized it, she was walking out with an entire role of toilet paper attached to and trailing behind her. It was everywhere in the bathroom. I asked her what happened and she said, "Who did that?"

On 1/18/02, Sarah was screened for a nursing home so I could put her on waiting lists. I asked when I put her to bed if she knew who I was. She said, "I don't know, but you take good care of me. I'll find out."

On 3/2/02, Sarah and I toured the assisted living facility that I had chosen. I felt like a traitor because I did it behind her back, while reassuring her that I would keep her at home forever. Sarah and I were introduced to everyone. As we were leaving, Sarah turned pale and froze at the front door. She looked into my eyes and said, "Please don't do this to me. I love you so much." That astounded me. I knew that I was not going to bring Sarah back the following Monday. We held hands and cried our eyes out after we left. I was in a trance because I found myself lost somewhere on the west end of Richmond. I had no idea where I was or how I got there. We eventually arrived home safely. We didn't talk to each other for the rest of the day. We sat and stared into space. When I regrouped psychologically, I called and reenrolled Sarah in the Adult Day Center at Lucy Corr. I cancelled her Monday reservation at the assisted living facility. I was back to square one!

On 9/15/02, Sarah was spaced more than unusual in her own world. She remained that way all day. As I was put her to bed, I asked her where she went during the day. She said, "It was very dark. There was no one there. It was like I was going to die."

On 12/22/02, Sarah passed out at the adult day center. Her facial muscles were loose and distorted. She was not able to raise her head and drooled. She had stroke like symptoms, so I rushed her to the emergency room. All tests were negative. Once again, there was no explanation for her episode.

On 2/6/03, I rushed Sarah to the emergency room. She was severely dehydrated because of the vomiting and diaherra that she had throughout the night. She was diagnosed with the noro-virus.

On 2/23/03, Sarah was rushed to the hospital again with the same symptoms. She was diagnosed with severe pancreatitis.

On 3/3/03, Sarah's ultra-sound indicated that she had severe gall stones necessitating the removal of her gall bladder.

On 3/21/03, Sarah's gall bladder was removed during a major surgical procedure.

On 3/27/03, Sarah was released to a local rehabilitation center from the hospital.

On 3/30/03, Tom, Sean, Bobby and Kathy arrived for a family meeting. They read me the riot act by saying, "We have already lost our mother; we do not want to lose you too. You need to do something now. You need to get help or place mom in a facility."

On 4/9/03, Sarah returned home. I recognized that she was different and would require more skilled care. I hired CNAs to take care of Sarah for the day shift, while I handled the night shift.

On 4/28/03, Sarah returned to the Adult Day Center at Lucy Corr Village.

Bobby read a poem to his mother at a Mother's Day Celebration 2003 at Lucy Corr. He wrote the poem specifically for his visit.

I'LL ALWAYS REMEMBER YOU
By Robert B. Schaefer Jr.

You kissed away my tears when I skinned a knee
You always cheered me up when bullies teased me.
You taught me to be honest and true to myself
Pampering me in sickness, nursing me to health.

I got your eyes, your smile, your zest for living
So much joy inside and a love for giving.
The gifts that you gave me are treasured in my heart
Whether we're together or a million miles apart.

I hope I've been a good son, one you're proud of
Caring and loving with strength from above.
You're always on my mind, in my heart and soul
Helping me to succeed to reach every goal.

I love you Mom please remember that phrase
Because you showed me how in so many ways.
At times it's tough, but I realize through and through
You may forget me sometimes, but I always remember you.

On 5/31/03, Sarah said, "Someone did something to me and I don't know what."

On 6/9/03, Sarah said, "You're a beautiful man," as I was putting her to bed.

LESSONS LEARNED

• Frenzy is the fourth milestone reached in the development of a care-partner.

• This is the most critical stage for the lion's share of care-partners.

• Wandering can become commonplace during this period. Enroll your loved one in the Alzheimer's Association Medic Alert/Safe Return Program and Project Lifesaver. These programs save lives.

• The average care-partner tends to go it alone during this stage of development.

• Care-partners will tend to ignore their own health and well being.

• Defense mechanisms protect care-partners for a period of time; Things are likely to change during this stage.

• Care-partners cannot outrun pain and discomfort forever; they must be acknowledged and addressed as part of this milestone.

• Dark, intrusive and scary thoughts can bother care-partners.

• Visions of in-home care, an adult day center, an assisted living facility or a nursing home are common stressors.

Chapter 6
I CAN TELL YOU WHAT TO DO, BUT
YOU MAKE YOUR OWN CHOICES

God, please help me. I don't know what to do anymore.
(Bob – 7/4/01)

Thinking outside the box can be your key to survival not only during the frenzy stage, but also throughout your career as a care-partner. By that I mean, finding an unorthodox rather than a logical solution for the behavior or situation that you are faced with. It is a skill to be mastered and put into action as early as possible. Keep your Alzheimer's detective, fisherman and/or hostage negotiator hats, as well as all of the others available to regularly bolster your competency and victories. This is of prime importance when the difficult and often unexplained behaviors try to get the better of you. These stressors will materialize when you are overburdened, overwhelmed, out of balance, burned out and barely able to see the forest through the trees.

There are no black and white or right and wrong answers when you deal with such episodes. Rather, they involve finding out what works best for you with the health and well-being of your loved one and you as a primary focus. I can tell you what to do, but you must make your own choices. No one else can think, be innovative or think outside the box for you. The ball is in your court. You control your own destiny. You have to be willing to take that first step which empowers you to think the unthinkable.

The following situations that Sarah and I faced during her progression led me to begin thinking differently and making my own choices based upon Sarah as an individual. I trained myself slowly to invent unorthodox solutions of common problems that attempted to destroy our peace and tranquility. We faced the unknown just as you are and will in the future. Taking a chance can be intimidating, but the results will be rewarding.

Look at our predicaments as if they were building blocks essential for your success. Some may pass into your journey and some may not. In either case, these experiences may give you ideas. If they do, you may master new ways to deal with old problems. Hopefully, they will motivate you to think with a positive attitude while putting your perseverance and creativity to work to negotiate the curves that lie in the road ahead.

PHYSICAL AILMENTS—Sarah injured herself frequently during the early stage of her progression. Once she started to limp. We thought that she might have sprained her ankle. The orthopedic surgeon discovered that Sarah had a stress fracture in two of her toes. He said that her injuries were the result of repeated trauma to her toes. We suspect that Sarah stubbed her toes frequently, but she forgot that she hurt herself. They were likely caused by the deterioration of her balance and depth perception.

Sarah was required to wear a special boot to protect and help her toes heal. That was a problem and challenge for the both of us because she refused daily to wear it. She forgot that she had injured her toes. Shortly after her toes healed, she tripped while walking the dog. She complained constantly about severe pain in her neck and back. Tests revealed that she suffered from degenerative disc disorder. She had surgery. Her recovery was slow and painful. She wore a neck brace until late in her progression at which time she forgot about her injury and the pain. She refused or forgot to wear the brace after that.

LOST IN OUR HOUSE—We moved from Virginia Beach to Richmond, VA when Sarah was in the middle stage. As anticipated, the move took its toll. She was not able to find her way around our new house. She got lost in our bedroom. If I asked her to go from the bedroom to the den, she couldn't do it. She could not find the bathroom when she needed it. That was frustrating for the both of us. To overcome this, I put brightly colored feet on the floor. I made paths from the kitchen and den to the bathroom, hoping that would help Sarah to find her way on her own. I also put large colorful signs with pictures on the doors leading to the bathroom and bedroom. These worked well because Sarah could find the bedroom and bathroom on her own. It raised her self-esteem, which was important. When it became too difficult for her to follow the steps and signs, I made up songs and jingles to keep her interested and challenged to use my cues. That was fun and kept us both laughing. What a life-saver until Sarah was no longer able to read or recognize them.

WANDERING AT NIGHT—I used a childproof cover on the inside of the bedroom doorknob. If I was in a deep sleep, the noise Sarah made trying to open the door was enough to wake me. I put deadbolts with keys on all doors leading outside the house. I kept them locked at all times and wore the key around my neck for quick access. I put a cheap battery operated alarm on the doors leading outside for the times when I didn't or forgot to lock the deadbolts. I am not a fan of medications, but Sarah's nighttime wandering was so bad and dangerous that I asked her doctor to prescribe an appropriate sleep aid. That made nights more tolerable, but didn't totally alleviate the problem.

VANISHING ON OUTINGS—Sarah managed to wander away from me at every store, park, or other location in our county. It took thirty seconds of distraction and she was gone. It was a scary situation. I discovered that purchasing and traveling with a wheelchair solved that problem. Sarah looked forward to and expected a ride. In the grocery store, I put a basket on her lap and put her in charge of the groceries. That kept her busy and raised her self esteem. She felt that she was doing something useful and important. She was enrolled in the Alzheimer's Safe Return/Medic Alert Program early in her progression. She never attempted to remove her bracelet.

I WANT TO GO HOME—Sarah went through a long period of sundowning during which she wanted to go home every evening. This included wandering, anxiety and agitation. It didn't matter to her that she was already at home. Telling her that she was home increased her anxiety and agitation and led to arguments. I thought outside the box whenever Sarah wanted to go home. I took her for a ride in the car with the hope that it would relax her. I returned home in half an hour and she would normally say, "Thank goodness we are finally home." That kept her content until the next evening when she started the cycle all over again. No amount of fussing, reasoning or explaining satisfied her desire to go home. Sarah has always loved to ride in a car so that helped. I found that any time that Sarah was agitated a ride in the car reduced it. It distracted her and solved a potential problem. On one occasion, Sarah came out of the bathroom in the morning with all of her toilet articles. I asked her what she was doing. She said, "I want to go home." Rather than arguing, we went for a ride. When we returned and I drove in the driveway, Sarah was satisfied. She was distracted long enough that she thought about something else. A ride in the car might be an inconvenience, but it is worth it, if it solves the behavior that you are facing.

CONSTANT REPETITION—Sarah repeated anything and everything for a period of time. She had a series of questions that she asked over and over again. What time is it? Are we going to church?

Who is coming for dinner tonight? Where are we going? – are a few examples. It baffled me that she remembered to ask the same questions over and over again; however, she was not able to recall what she had eaten for breakfast or where we had just been or what we had just done. I never found a satisfactory answer to make the repetition totally disappear. There is no magic formula; however, I came up with a unique answer to Sarah's questions. I tried to divert her attention in a funny way. I made up lyrics to songs to encourage her to laugh. That did the trick and helped prevent either of us both from losing our cool. It took effort and ingenuity, but it was well worth it. At times, nothing worked and it meant that I had to turn her questions off. I let her ask and ask, but I didn't respond. I threw out an occasional yes or no and that kept her happy. Remember, it is an individual thing. It is thinking 'outside the box' to satisfy your loved one based upon your knowledge of them. On occasion, I'd accepted the challenge by answering the same question in different way. My goal was to divert her attention with the hope that she would stop the repetition. I suspect that Sarah enjoyed my mind games because she never got upset with me. If she was happy, I was happy. That thought is a good motivator.

EVERYDAY ANXIETY– Sarah was easily bored in the middle stage. Naturally, that made her anxious and irritable. She recognized that she was losing abilities in many areas; which caused her to feel insecure and embarrassed. At the time of her diagnosis and into the early stage, Sarah spent hours reading, playing bridge, working on puzzles, or doing crossword puzzles and crypto quotes. As those disappeared, she listened to music or watched television constantly. When she was no longer able to concentrate on television, she tried to help me more with the household chores.

I tried to keep her busy with other tasks like putting clothes or groceries away. When all else failed, Sarah folded laundry over and over again until she wanted to take a nap. That again gave her a sense of accomplishment and boosted her self esteem, which is what she needed.

Soft or oldies music tended to reduce Sarah's anxiety level. Music was a life saver when everything else failed, especially in the middle of the night. Sarah stood and rocked back and forth in front of the television for hours with the oldies blaring away. I combined a long walk for exercise with the music, especially afternoons to tire her out for bedtime. Exercise also diverted her attention whenever the anxiety level increased.

AGITATION LEADING TO VIOLENT BEHAVIOR—I considered myself to be lucky as a care partner. Sarah did not have a tendency to be violent, but that could be a concern for some care partners. As you well know, as Alzheimer's progresses, the ability of your loved one to communicate diminishes. They may not be able to verbalize that they are in pain or feeling some type of discomfort. The most common ailment that causes a dementia patient to lash out or become violent is a urinary tract infection (UTI). A UTI may cause a dementia patient to attack their care-partner verbally or physically. If the UTI is treated with antibiotics, the abnormal behavior will likely disappear as the infection disappears. On occasion, aggressive behavior might require prescription medications although I prefer that is a last resort. You should be aware of that. Once again, put your Alzheimer's detective hat on to zero in on and determine the source of behavioral changes, especially if they are sudden.

HANDICAPPED PARKING—Sarah's doctor completed a form that I hand-carried to the Department of Motor Vehicle to secure a handicapped parking placard for our car. I was able to park closer to events, stores, and offices. This was especially important as Sarah's depth perception, balance and gait interfered with her ability to walk any distance within a reasonable amount of time.

BATHING—I was able to bathe Sarah in a tub well into the middle stage of her progression without any problem. All of a sudden, the rising water made her anxious and I stopped baths. I replaced baths with showers. They worked for a period of time until the stream of water coming out of the shower-head frightened her. I played soothing music in the background, which calmed her during showers for a little longer. I took off the traditional shower head and replaced it with a long shower extension that permitted me to spray a soft stream of water directly onto her head for shampooing and then to specific parts of the body for washing. By doing that, Sarah was not overwhelmed by the hard stream of water spraying over her entire body at the same time. That combination enabled me to continue to shower her with a minimal amount of anxiety. I introduced a plastic stool for her to sit on which continued to make her comfortable and less anxious. I stopped the background music and replaced it with my singing to her. I didn't sing traditional songs that we both knew, but made up songs and used Sarah's name in the lyrics. That amused and distracted her for many additional nights. I was willing to do anything to get through the bathing routine without raising her anxiety level.

EATING AT RESTURANTS—Sarah and I wanted to live normal lives as long as that was possible. She always enjoyed eating dinner out. We didn't go out often, but I noticed that when we did people stared at her because her eating skills deteriorated. That infuriated me. My first reaction was to embarrass those staring at her, but I decided that was not a good idea. I thought outside the box and made up cards on the computer. They pointed out that Sarah had Alzheimer's disease. I mentioned that she was a kind, loving, caring and considerate person whose skills and abilities were being taken away by this horrendous disease. I asked that they not stare at her. I put my telephone number on the card and suggested that they call if they wanted to learn more about Alzheimer's disease. I thanked them for their cooperation. Passing those cards not only made me feel better, but it helped to spread the word about Alzheimer's disease in a positive way.

EATING AT HOME—Sarah was a good eater. However, as the disease progressed, there was a gradual decline in her interest in food. With my Alzheimer's detective hat on, I noticed that Sarah was frustrated while eating because she was not able to use her fork or spoon. She dropped the food off them or accidently pushed it onto the table before she was able to eat it. Everything spilled on the table or floor. She did not want to ask for help. I put her food into a deeper dish so that she could use the sides of it to push her food onto the spoon or fork more easily. That worked for a while. I used a divided plate with at least three separate compartments. That also worked for a short while. Eventually, I gave her more finger foods so that she did not have to bother with a fork or spoon. When she reached the stage of having to be fed and her appetite decreased, I stimulated her taste buds with some type of a sweet before giving her the food itself. I used ice cream, and puddings to start with and eventually sugar when those didn't work any longer. When she couldn't eat regular food even if it was pureed, I fed her pudding, ice cream and thick shakes with crushed bananas for nourishment.

BEAUTY SALON APPOINTMENTS—Sarah was very anxious when she got her a haircut because she realized that she was not able to talk or follow instructions like she had done in the past. To adapt to that, I stayed with Sarah during her appointments. When we arrived at the beauty parlor or wherever, I discretely handed the beautician a card to let her know what she could expect from her. This is a sample of those cards:

Please be patient with Sarah…

She was diagnosed with Alzheimer's disease at a young age. She requires a few extra minutes of your time because she has difficulty holding a conversation and following instructions. She becomes anxious if I leave her, so I will stay with her until you have finished. Her feelings and emotions are intact, so it is important not to talk about or around her. Thank you for your patience and cooperation.

DRIVERS LICENSE—I asked Sarah to surrender her driver's license when it was obvious that she was getting lost and having difficulty. She admitted getting lost on several occasions. That scared me. Sarah was unusual because she surrendered her license to me without any problem at all. I sent it to Department of Motor Vehicles (DMV). They sent Sarah a complementary thank you letter that I framed and mounted on a wall for her to look at. She was proud of that letter. I obtained an identification card which is available in Virginia. If she had not surrendered her license, I would have requested that her doctor notify DMV. If that did not happen, I would have asked the doctor write a note on a prescription form indicating that Sarah should stop driving. Sarah respected her doctors and would follow their instructions without hesitation. As a last resort, I was prepared to request that Sarah be retested to prevent her from hurting herself or any other person on the highway.

DOCTOR APPOINTMENTS—Sarah couldn't sit quietly in a doctor's office for any period of time. I let the nurses know that fact and requested her appointments be scheduled either as the first or last appointment of the day or before or after lunch. The nursing staff cooperated with this unique request. I rescheduled an appointment if for some reason there was a long wait.

I wrote a summary of Sarah's and my concerns and gave it to the nurse so the doctor could review it prior to examining her. By doing that, we did not talk about Sarah in her presence. Both of those ideas helped to keep Sarah's anxiety at a minimal level. Here is a sample of the letter that I prepared for the doctor:

Dr…

Sarah has been having difficulties. She overheard me discussing them with our daughter on the telephone last evening and became hysterical. She gets frustrated and anxious whenever I talk about her in front of her, so from this visit on, I will be giving you a summary of our concerns in a note so that you can review them before talking to Sarah.

Sarah was awake and wandering at 2:00 am Monday morning. She was in a trance, but she followed me around the house telling me that she was scared and sorry, but she didn't know why. Sarah was awake at 4:00 am Tuesday morning. I told her that I was going to work on the computer. She stayed in bed, but she was awake the entire time. She has no appetite at breakfast and dinner, although she has been eating at the adult day center. She has severe burps/hiccups before and after meals and frequently during the day. She had a bad attack before dinner Tuesday evening. I gave her water and Rolaids. Her face was flushed and she acted very anxious and as if she was going to pass out. She felt better after fifteen minutes, but refused to eat dinner. Could Exelon be causing these reactions? Her quality of life is not good. I reported that she fainted again at 7:30 am on 5/12/01, as she was coming out of the bedroom. I elevated her feet and she was okay after fifteen minutes. This is the fourth time that she has passed out, but tests have not determined what is causing these episodes. I am especially interested in solving her wandering during the night. It is getting more and more difficult to recover from the loss of sleep. Thank you for listening.

EMERGENCY ROOM VISITS—It is absolutely necessary to carry the following documents with you at all times: a copy of any medical directives, a power of attorney and a list of all medications. I also prepared a letter specifically for doctors and emergency room visits. This letter was drafted to assure that Sarah and I are not separated during any tests or medical procedures. This happened on a previous occasion and Sarah's anxiety level reached unbelievable heights. She was subjected to a number of tests, one of which I considered barbaric. They were done without anyone's permission. This is that letter:

I, ROBERT B. SCHAEFER, residing at _____, am the full-time care partner and power of attorney for my wife, SARAH P. SCHAEFER, date of birth _____, Social Security Number_____. SARAH was diagnosed with the probable early onset of Alzheimer's disease 15 years ago. She has a difficult time communicating with strangers and it is a struggle for a nurse or physician who does not know her to determine if she is in any type of pain or discomfort. SARAH is very sensitive to, but normally not able to respond to her surroundings. She becomes extremely anxious and upset whenever she is separated from me for any reason.

In order to assure that her rights and dignity are preserved, I request that I be present during any office visits, examinations and/or consults and have full access to her medical records. I will present a copy of her Power of Attorney upon request.

Please note that I will not authorize payments under her primary or secondary insurance carriers unless these conditions are met.

Sincerely,

ROBERT B. SCHAEFER

HOSPITAL ADMISSIONS – Be prepared to have overnight stays at the hospital after falls, injuries or surgeries. Some hospitals require a family member to stay with an Alzheimer's/dementia patient 24/7. Notify family members and friends in advance, so they can assist you at such times. Sarah stayed for ten days following major surgery for the removal of her diseased gall bladder. We had to assure that a family member stayed with her during that critical time. Fortunately, our children divided the ten days with me in shifts that prevented anyone from burning out or being overwhelmed. Understand that anesthesia could exacerbate the progression of the dementia. That occurred following Sarah's surgery.

NEIGHBORS—The time arrived when it was appropriate to notify our neighbors about Sarah's diagnosis. I felt that it was necessary because of the bizarre behavior of one of our neighbor's.

Sarah walked Skipper one afternoon. She came home hysterical after fifteen minutes. She told me that a man on the next block screamed at her because she had let Skipper relieve himself on his lawn on a regular basis. I knew that that was not true because I watched Sarah regularly. I also wanted to reach out and enlist the support and cooperation of my neighbors. This is that letter:

February 2000

Dear Neighbor:

Now that spring is on the way and we will be spending more time outdoors, I will share some thoughts with those of you who we have the most frequent contact. This is difficult so bear with me.

Sarah and I have lived in our ranch for a year. We moved to Birkdale to be closer to and seek the support of our children, three of whom reside in this area. We relocated because Sarah was diagnosed with the probable early onset of Alzheimer's disease, while she was in her forties. That was ten years ago. I worked until 1996, when I retired to become Sarah's care-partner. Unfortunately, the move has taken its toll and Sarah is not as able to hide the signs of her illness, as cleverly as she was able to do. I take care of Sarah 24/7. I do not tell you this to elicit sympathy, but rather to help you understand our situation. We don't want to be labeled as the strange people on the corner.

Sarah has always had a pleasant and outgoing personality. The doctors say that those traits helped her to function well and hide her symptoms; however, those traits are declining to the point that Sarah relies upon me to help her do everything. She is still outgoing and loves to be with people, but at times words don't come to her during conversations. Naturally, that embarrasses her. Sarah's feelings and emotions are alive and well!

Some of you have been kind enough to invite us to social gatherings or to join groups. We have declined, not because we are anti-social, but because it has become much more difficult for us to socialize. I have learned that even social gatherings with our children and grandchildren can be overwhelming. She wants to do and say the right thing in all situations, which raises her stress level and makes it even more difficult for her to communicate

I am sharing this with you because you may have wondered about things that Sarah said during a conversation, or you might have seen her picking up leaves on the lawn by hand. You have all seen Sarah walking Skipper. I watch them very closely and have been forced to take over the morning and evening walks because I just don't feel comfortable letting her do that alone. She thrives on that responsibility, so I let her continue to do it during the day. I mention this to prevent any neighbor from yelling at or disciplining Sarah for letting our dog walk on their lawn. This happened recently and I would like to avoid a repeat of that. If Sarah ever causes a problem, come to me and I will solve the problem. Sarah is not a danger to anyone except herself. She has daily contact with our grandchildren and they all gravitate to her and love her to death. It is as if they understand what is happening and they try their best to make Sarah feel comfortable and at home.

I hope and pray that all of you will continue to feel the same toward Sarah. She is hanging on to her memory with every bit of strength that she has available. Please talk to her when you see her and be patient if it takes her a minute to respond. If you ever see Sarah walking Skipper and she appears to be wandering away from our home, please turn her back in the right direction or let me know immediately. She is working hard to keep you all from knowing that anything is wrong.

Thank you for listening. I hope that this information does not change your feelings toward us. Finally, please remember us the both in your prayers.

Sincerely and God Bless,
ROBERT B. SCHAEFER

A couple of months after I distributed it to our neighbors it paid off. Sarah went three consecutive nights without sleeping. I was exhausted trying to keep up with her. One afternoon, I put the oldies station on the television to entertain Sarah. She sat down on the couch next to me and fell asleep. That was the last thing that I remembered until the telephone rang. A neighbor called to tell me that Sarah was walking down a path on the golf course behind his house. I rushed out was able to find Sarah before she got away or lost.

TELEPHONE—I purchased a big telephone with large letters and numbers so that Sarah was able to read them. This made it easier for her to put the receiver on the cradle after she was done talking. The telephone was a major stressor for her.

TRAVELING—Sarah and I loved to travel and wanted to do so for as long as we could. The following are a few hints that helped us to have better and more organized trips:

Restrooms: When planning a long trip, make sure that you know where the restrooms are along the way. This is important should any type of an emergency arise. If possible, identify unisex or family restrooms, so that you will be able to go in with your loved one when that time arrives. We traveled before unisex or family restrooms became popular. I was forced to approach a female traveler on one occasion to assist me in locating Sarah when she did not come out of the ladies room. I thought outside the box. I laminated a sign that I prepared on the computer. I used it on rare occasions to close the ladies room. I did that to accompany Sarah in the restroom and assist her with her needs. I made the sign look fancy and professional with illustrations. It was more appropriate to use the sign on the ladies room because they were more understanding and tolerant of our situation. Here is that sign:

ATTENTION

The ladies room will be closed for the next few minutes so that I can assist my wife with her personal needs. This is necessary because of her diagnosis of the probable early onset of Alzheimer's disease. She is not able to take care of herself without assistance from me as her full-time care partner. I apologize for any inconvenience and appreciate your understanding and patience.

This prop was a life-saver on trips. We had one mishap to show how important it was. We were driving back from Florida. I stopped at a rest area. Sarah went in the ladies room, while I stood guard at the entrance and waited for her. After ten minutes, I started worrying because she had not come out. I called her, but she did not answer. There was no attendant or other woman entering or leaving. I was about to go in to find her when a woman arrived. I explained my situation and asked if she would look for Sarah. She came out in seconds and told me that the restroom was empty. She told me that there was also an exit leading to the southbound side, which she probably used when she was disoriented. I panicked and searched the southbound side. I found Sarah in tears fifteen minutes later in the truck parking area. Words cannot describe the panic and fear I felt. I realize that I made a mistake by not asking for help immediately because I had lost valuable time. Do not ever make that same mistake. Time is of essence whenever you lose a loved one with dementia. Call for help immediately. It was after that incident that I prepared my laminated placard to close a restroom for an emergency.

CLOTHING – It is of paramount importance when traveling to always take a change of clothing for emergencies.

GLASSES, NECK-BRACE & PURSES: Sarah needed to wear glasses and a neck brace. She was not able to function without either. As her Alzheimer's progressed, she lost her glasses daily. Travel with a spare pair of glasses. Some type of a tether should reduce the losses. The neck brace Sarah worn started to disappear as often as her glasses. I made sure that I had a spare of both on any trip. She also insisted on carrying a purse with her at all times. She lost that every time that we took a trip. I removed everything of value from it to include credit cards, money, checks. I did that without her knowledge and I made sure that I put other worthless papers and documents in their place. It pays to be innovative and proactive. Think ahead and outside the box. Any loss was devastating to Sarah, so it was important to keep her happy by replacing lost items with a spare as soon as it was possible.

MEDICATIONS: Always travel with extra medications. Make sure that you are in charge of those medications and their distribution.

JEWELRY: Sarah did not wear a lot of jewelry, but I was concerned about her diamond engagement ring that contained an expensive and treasured family diamond. Sarah reached the point that she would take it off nights while traveling and she would not remember to put it on the next morning. On occasion, it accidently slipped off her finger during the night. It was panic time trying to find it in the bedding, if she remembered that it was missing. She would not part with that ring for any reason. My solution was to tell her that I had to take it to the jewelers to have the prongs on her diamond tightened. I asked that jeweler replace the real diamond with a clear glass stone that would resemble the original. I returned the ring to Sarah with the glass replica of her diamond. That was a major stress reducer because her diamond was safely tucked away at home.

LOSING EVERDAY ITEMS—Sarah regularly lost or misplaced most of her things to include keys, glasses, neck brace, wallet, credit cards, money, checkbook, purses, coats, hats, gloves, engagement ring, puzzle books, television remote, and portable telephone. Something was always missing. It was a constant source of frustration for the both of us. Sarah's anxiety level rose tenfold whenever she searched for one of her lost things.

WRISTWATCH: Sarah loved to wear a wrist watch. She was obsessed with knowing what time it was. She checked and rechecked her watch for the time. It became more difficult and frustrating for her to read the numbers on her watch. I bought every cheap watch that I could with larger and larger numbers. As she lost the ability to tell time on a conventional watch, I went digital. That helped for a while, but she eventually lost the ability to tell time.

CONSTANT PICKING AT PARTS OF THE BODY: Be aware that it is not unusual for dementia patients to pick at parts of their body as part of their progression.

FAMILY GATHERINGS: Family gatherings for birthdays, anniversaries, and holidays can overwhelm or over stimulate your loved one. This is most common during the later stages of dementia. I learned this the hard way. Our four children and ten grandchildren gathered for a celebration on Sarah's birthday. I thought it would be exciting to have our entire family for ice cream and cake. What a mistake! Sarah could not cope with the noise and confusion. Her anxiety level soared as she let me know that she had to escape from the commotion. Once I took her into the silence of her bedroom her anxiety level lowered. That was sad because Sarah loved her children and grandchildren. She wanted to be with them more than anything else. My solution involved having one family visit at a time, which solved the problem.

COSMETICS—Sarah insisted that she have lipstick with her at all times. She was constantly putting it on. Naturally, she also lost it on a regular basis. The loss of her lipstick drove her crazy. She couldn't do anything else until she had lipstick back in her possession. The secret was to keep plenty on hand, so that as soon as she lost one, it could be quickly replaced.

PARANOIA—Sarah was very paranoid during the middle stage. I had to be in her sight every moment of the day and night. She felt that I was going to leave her or put her in a nursing home because of her Alzheimer's. I could not to talk on the telephone without her thinking that I was making arrangements to get rid of her. If I left the room to change my clothes or take a shower or go to the restroom, Sarah was behind me like a shadow. She just stood and stared at me. It was annoying because I didn't have any privacy at all.

COLDS—A simple cold can be a major issue and stressor for a dementia patient and their care partner. Any infection can be disruptive and lead to anxiety or annoying behaviors. Sarah's nose ran constantly when she had a cold. She had to be reminded to wipe her nose. Whenever she did she dropped the used tissues on the floor or stuck them in the cushion of her chair. I set a wastepaper basket next to her, but she would still throw them on the floor. She didn't see or recognize it even when I pointed it out to her. She forgot what she was supposed to do with the used tissues.

FALLING—Sarah fell on a regular basis as she progressed through the middle stage. This was so true when she got up in the middle of the night to use the bathroom. Her loss of balance, eyesight and depth perception contributed to this. She had gait that caused her to trip or lose her balance on occasion. Stairs were another source of falls. I had to be aware of possible hazards such as lighting, rugs and debris on the floor. I did whatever I thought was necessary to prevent her from falling and injuring herself.

AGNOSIA—is the inability to recognize familiar people and things. This usually appears during the middle stage. Sarah was confused about everything in the house. If I asked her to put something away, she was no longer was able to match an object or a thing with a word such as closet, cabinet, or drawer.

FOLLOWING INSTRUCTIONS—I've already talked about the difficulties that Sarah had getting into a car. Another example was asking Sarah to pick up Skipper's favorite toy from under the coffee table. She had no idea what I was talking about even though she was staring at it a foot away. Sarah could not follow any instructions, so the secret was to try not to give her any.

FAINTING SPELLS—Sarah was plagued with frequent and random fainting spells. I had a tendency to panic when the earlier fainting spells occurred. I attribute most of that to the fact that I thought that she might be having mini-strokes. Initially, Sarah was transported to the emergency room because she recovered so slowly. She was given every test and wore a heart monitor, but no cause was found. It was eventually decided that they were due to the use of the cholinesterase inhibitors. I became more and more accustomed to these spells and treated her without panic according to instructions given to me by the doctor.

LESSONS LEARNED

• Thinking outside the box will not solve all of your problems, but it will make life more tolerable.

• Being innovative and proactive can help you to stay on the road to survival.

• I can tell you what to do, but you must make your own choices.

Chapter 7
TOLERANCE

Sarah said, "I wish we could be together again at home."
(8/3/03), "I should be able to take care of myself."
(9/1/03), and "I want to go home." (9/11/03)

The final milestone that a care-partner is likely to reach during his journey is tolerance. Theoretically, this should be the best, most balanced and pleasant stretch for the majority of care-partners. It will normally come into being at some point during the latter part of the middle stage of progression. The average care-partner will likely be overwhelmed because of the physical and mental demands generated throughout the frenzy stage. As you have seen, stress has been a major component of all the periods of development, but normally reaches its high point during the previous milestone.

I ignored one important aspect of life that constantly puts survival at risk. Stress affects everyone who is battling Alzheimer's. I realized during this final developmental span that I had to be proactive and do something to control my stress level. It was the first time on this journey that I actually had the time or inclination to acknowledge its impact and take positive steps to bring life back into some semblance of balance again. It was no longer appropriate to ignore the early warning signs which had become second nature.

As a young stress instructor, I developed a number of symptoms to gauge how well I or anyone was handling the stressors of life. The following is that list:

EARLY WARNING SIGNS OF STRESS
1. Change of personality
2. Isolation from support groups
3. Unusual sleep patterns
4. Continued somatic (physical) symptoms
5. Excessive use of self-medication
6. Nothing seems pleasurable

Most of you are familiar with these because you have experienced some or all of them in the past. I feel confident saying that the majority of care-partners probably ignored these signs throughout the first four periods of development. I did for an extended period of time. There was little time, strength, energy, or desire to face them in the wake of the staggering responsibilities that you were already saddled with. It is common to exhibit some of these symptoms when facing certain stressors. The key is to recognize when these markers remain and plague you for weeks, months, or years rather than a day or two. Train yourself and your body to recognize when they become long rather than short term visitors. If symptoms persist listen to your body when it sounds the alarm.

A basic understanding of stress and how it affects you, your body and performance is essential, if you choose, to use it to your advantage. Stress is the rate of wear and tear on the human body caused by living. You are always under some level of stress as long as you are alive. Stress is either positive or negative. Positive stress normally lasts for a short period of time and can beneficial to the body. Negative stress lingers and can seek out the weakest link in your body to wreak havoc. A traumatic incident or other crisis will initiate the fight or flight stress reaction. The body gets hit with a biochemical blitz. Countless chemicals and hormones release into the bloodstream and results in the body being out of balance. It is our job to restore balance, which will in turn reduce the stress level.

We give meaning to the stressors that we face through our perceptions. Coping with stress often requires that we change our perceptions. This is especially true in those situations wherein you have no control over the stressor. It goes without saying that we have no control over the progression of Alzheimer's. That is tough to grasp and heed, but the ability to change your perceptions is key to survival in this helping role.

The life of a care-partner isn't glamorous or exciting. At times, stress will be disruptive and unbearable. It can lead to negativism and depression, which is a waste of time and effort. No amount of worry will change the path of this disease; yet, we tend to forget and deny that reality. Care-partners need to monitor their stress as it is common to ignore the early warning signs.

Happiness is a choice. No one can make you happy unless you are willing to be happy. The problem is that the average care-partner sees no reason to be happy with the burden that they are facing. I felt that way until I was absorbed with the fact that it was okay to be happy. Life is much easier with a positive attitude. Negativism will burn you out and lead to your defeat. The ball is in your court. Your attitude and perceptions will determine your fate. Look for your own motivator. One of mine has always been thinking about the ten most important words that I ever learned. Those are – 'if it is to be, it is up to me.'

To assist further, I have included a list of common sense ways to keep your stress within your own tolerance limits. Debrief yourself daily, monitor your stress barometer and practice some or all of the following suggestions routinely to live a more meaningful life. Channel time and energy into the positive rather than negative. Avoid the most destructive emotion that will try to overwhelm you. That is self-pity.

• Realize and understand your limitations as a care-partner. Acknowledge sooner than later that you should ask for help.
• Attend and become involved in a church if that is in your background.
• Remember that you still have your own life to live. Live it to the fullest—that is what your loved one expects of you.
• Seek daily respite through an adult day center, family member, friend or professional care-giver.
• Eat a well-balanced diet, get adequate natural sleep and monitor your health through an annual physical examination.
• Exercise regularly.
• Have a good sense of humor—it is okay to laugh.
• Use relaxation exercises as appropriate.
• Volunteer at an organization such as the Alzheimer's Association.
• Work part-time as appropriate, to stay involved outside of your role as a care-partner.
• Socialize with family and friends often.
• Find time for a hobby that is pleasurable.
• Educate yourself and develop the mindset that an assisted living or a nursing home may be appropriate or necessary in the future.
• Keep a journal or diary to debrief yourself daily, especially if you do not have a friend or confidant.
• And last but not least, if you feel that you are losing control of your emotions in spite of your efforts, seek professional help. There is no stigma involved in helping yourself—A healthy person that seeks help.

Tolerance should begin to bring peace to your life. A better understanding and open-mindedness toward your responsibilities will also develop. Pieces to the puzzle of dementia should fall into place although it will never totally be understood or completed. A new drive and attitude will become obvious. Some degree of acceptance will begin to appear. You will better understand the reason for your calling and struggles.

Isolation will be recognized and avoided as a negative stressor. Important and necessary decisions made will help you to appreciate that surviving depends heavily upon your attitude and mentality. Faith and love will prompt you to reach out for assistance from others. This can be reached in a number of ways.

The first path might involve keeping your loved one at home. This becomes easier with the continued support of family, friends and a professional home health agency. This is the most desired scenario for care-partners. It definitely was for me, but I was not able to make that happen. Some will be able to keep their loved ones at home without any or a minimal amount of outside assistance, especially if they have some type of formal training in health care. However, most will require some assistance.

The second path sets the use of full-time home health care professionals or private nurses in to motion within the home. This will be expensive. Not all care-partners can afford this luxury. Long-term care insurance would be beneficial, but it is not always available due to the cost. All too often, we tend to put off purchasing such coverage because of the mindset that it will never be needed. Naturally, we are healthy and bordering on invincible at that time of our lives. I know that at a younger age I never entertained thoughts about long-term care insurance for that reason.

The last and most difficult option involves placement in a long-term care facility, which is expensive unless you are fortunate enough to have long-term care insurance. Assisted living is private pay, while nursing homes will normally have limited Medicaid beds available.

Sarah moved to an assisted living facility on 7/23/03. Slowly but surely I adjusted to my new life. I compared placing Sarah in assisted living to putting our first born on a school bus for the first time. It was a difficult, but necessary and required act. We sorely missed him, but realized that it was in his best interests to attend school. It assured his continued education, development, socialization and maturity. The initial shock of losing Sarah was devastating; however, as time passed, I recognized that it was necessary for her health, well-being and survival.

Fellow care-partners in my support group and friends at the Alzheimer's Association warned me to expect changes in Sarah's behavior after she lived away from me for a period of time. I took in what they had to say but, didn't worry about it. Sarah did adapt well to her new surroundings. In fact, she was very close to her new caregivers to the point that she listened to them before me. I felt hurt initially, but that eventually reinforced the fact that I had made the right decision at the right time. She was no longer dependant on me. Sarah's demeanor and body language told me that she knew I was there for her daily visits. She seemed to anticipate and expect my visits. That was my first giant step into the tolerance leg of my journey.

My role shifted to that of care-manager to oversee Sarah's care, which is also stressful. Letting go of my former responsibilities was a difficult and gradual process. I had to believe and accept that others in the world that were capable of caring for Sarah with tender loving care. When I absorbed and agreed with that premise a calmness, patience, and open-mindedness surfaced and reinforced that I was entering the tolerance step. This was something that I never dreamed would ever or could happen. I shifted gears and was able to look at things differently.

As I transitioned into the tolerance leg, I made use of several simple steps that really enhanced our communication process. They can easily be overlooked because of their simplicity. I will mention them as another possible tool that will prevent you from having to reinvent the wheel.

My first recommendation is to keep everything as simple as you can. Consider the KISS principle by keeping it short and simple. Communicate with your loved one in the simplest, shortest, and most basic ways, which will help them to better process what you are trying to accomplish. Always strive to boost self-esteem without losing patience, getting angry, belittling or degrading. Too often, we do not consciously acknowledge our loved one's deterioration and losses. We should compensate for losses without it becoming an additional source of stress. For example, Sarah loved to go to dinner. She was not able to read the menu or make decisions. To avoid embarrassing her, I selected two items that I knew she liked and she chose one of them. That took the stress and embarrassment out of the process. Sarah felt special and her self-esteem level rose. We become so stressed that we miss the simplest of solutions to many of the problems that we face. Keep life as simple as possible by limiting choices and decisions.

The second hint is to move slowly and methodically. Recognize communication difficulties by speaking slowly and clearly. Make sure that every word is absorbed and processed. This will naturally take time, effort and patience, all of which may be in short supply. Half of the battle involves making sure that your message is received and processed. I presented everything to Sarah in small, slow steps. I always maintained eye contact while communicating. If Sarah processed the first item, if necessary, I tried a second short, slow detail. It was so much easier and professional than yelling or shouting instructions that were too complex and fast for her to understand. As a result, we remained calm and in most instances, Sarah understood and followed through on my instructions.

Another clue would have you show your loved one by example what you want them to do. That is so much more effective than rattling off instructions that are often too complex or misunderstood. It is common to skip or ignore this suggestion. Doing what you've always done in the past is easier and makes more sense; however, that disregards the deterioration that has likely occurred. Why learn something new? I used this technique to get Sarah into the car. Not accepting the fact that your loved one has changed will make this step difficult for some.

The final suggestion is to always wear a happy face. This will rub some the wrong way because they cannot find anything to smile about. I found that a happy face has a soothing effect especially when you are expected to be stressed and frustrated. Our loved one's can develop a sixth sense which permits them in the late stages to read our emotions. A genuine and sincere happy face goes a long way toward lessening or preventing catastrophic reactions.

Sarah's progression continued as I was making progress in the tolerance milestone. The photographs in the center section show Sarah's journey through the world of Alzheimer's until her death.

On 8/31/03, Sarah was mumbling during my visit. All of a sudden she said, "I wish we could be together again at home. I was shocked because she still processing and making sense of her surroundings.

On 9/1/03, Sarah was mumbling again. She reinforced her awareness when she said, "I should be able to take care of myself."

On 9/11/03, Sarah said, "You're good for me."

On 1/17/04, Sarah was anxious. She paced and wanted to go somewhere or do something. She mumbled that something was stupid.

On 1/31/04, Sarah was very anxious. It appeared to me as if she was recalling and possibly reliving her four miscarriages. She appeared to be experiencing physical pain.

On 4/5/04, Sarah began taking buspirone (Buspar) for severe anxiety and agitation.

On 5/29/04, Sarah continues to be anxious and agitated and mumbling, "I don't want to do this."

On 6/6/04, Sarah was anxious and agitated and kept saying "Let's go—go—go—go—come on…

On 9/3/04, Sarah looked me right in the eyes and said, "I like you."

On 10/12/04, Sarah grabbed my hand and said, "I love you."

On 10/24/04, Sarah was pacing as she became increasingly anxious and agitated. She said, "I'm going to kill myself.' I immediately hugged her, took her hand and walked with her. I reassured her that things would get better and I would be there to help and support her. That diverted her attention and calmed her down.

Conditions began to deteriorate at Sarah's new location. One of the better employees resigned due to a medical condition. Her work was dumped onto the remaining CNA. She bathed, dressed, toileted, groomed and fed all ten residents. She dispensed medications, cooked three meals a day and cleaned entire facility. Her day began at 6:00am and ended when she put her last resident to bed at 9:00pm.

She slept in a bedroom on the second floor for up to seven days a week. Several CNAs were hired to assist this employee, but when they saw what was expected of them daily, they disappeared.

I learned by accident that when this lone CNA left for a day or two, the administrator did not hire another CNA to replace her. Instead, she took a baby monitor home to listen for activity during the nighttime hours. She lived in a house next to the facility and felt that she could hear whenever a problem arose. I found this unacceptable. I put my Alzheimer's detective hat on to establish a pattern showing when the monitor was used. I planned to notify Social Services and /or Adult Protective Services (APS) on a night when I was sure that the residents were alone. Unfortunately, an unknown person reported this practice to Social Services. APS conducted a surprise late evening inspection only to find that the regular CNA was on the premises.

Life for me with the administrator was very strained. She looked for any and every excuse to get rid of Sarah. I documented problems that I noted with feeding, communicating, toileting, falls, and activities. She eventually notified me that Sarah was total care and would have to be moved. I wasn't happy because I feared that might accelerate Sarah's progression. I moved Sarah to the Clover Hill Neighborhood at Lucy Corr Village in Chesterfield, Virginia, within the next several weeks. Lucy Corr was thirteen miles from home which was a plus.

On 4/29/05, Sarah became a resident in the Clover Hill Neighborhood at Lucy Corr Village in Chesterfield, VA.

On 9/23/05, I noticed that Sarah is being kept in her wheelchair because of frequent falls and episodes of syncope.

On 5/14/06, Dr. Arline Bohannon advised that Sarah had pneumonia.

On 5/22/06, Sarah was enrolled in Hospice.

On 5/25/06, Hospice recommended that Sarah start a soft diet because of difficulty swallowing.

On 6/21/07, Hospice recommended that Sarah use a thickener for all liquids since she is having a difficult time swallowing.

On 1/14/08, hospice ordered morphine for Sarah, so that it would be available if needed.

On 1/16/08, Sarah tried to walk. She fell backwards without warning and flailed her arms. She yelled, "Its happening." I was able to get her into a lounge chair. She passed out and was put to bed for the remainder of the day.

On 4/1/08, Sarah remained in bed because of chest congestion and a runny nose.

For April through July 2008, Sarah ate less and less of her puree diet. On occasion, we cleaned food out of her mouth that she was not able to swallow. Her anxiety level stays high. Episodes of syncope occur daily; she drools during them. Blood pressure readings have been low, for example, 67/47. Pulse rate increases while she is passed out and there has been an irregular heartbeat.

On 7/21/08, Sarah was pale and extremely anxious. All of a sudden Sarah yelled, "I won't go!"

On 8/6/08, Sarah tried to stand, but she was far too weak. Her body started to shake as if she was having a seizure. Her mouth opened and she stopped breathing. I ran out of the room to find the charge nurse. By the time that I returned with the nurse, Sarah was breathing, but still unconscious. Blood pressure was 172/96 with a pulse rate of 80.

On 8/19/08, a seizure caused her body to shake. Her head snapped and rested on her chest, while she was unconscious.

On 9/1/08, Sarah passed out again while eating lunch.

On 10/ 6/08, Sarah was sick to her stomach. She was put to bed immediately. She threw up for an hour.

On 11/4/08, Sarah was unconscious and not able to get out of bed. She had difficulty breathing and started on oxygen.

On 11/10-12, 2008, Dr. Bohannon and Ms. Nixon made frequent trips to check Sarah. They stopped Remeron and Buspar and prescribed Ativan and morphine for her comfort.

On 11/13/08, my sister and our youngest son Bobby visited Sarah. Bobby brought his new daughter Mikayla, our eleventh grandchild, to meet Sarah. She was semi-conscious Dr. Bohannon adjusted her medications for pain and comfort.

November 2008—Sarah remains in bed. I stay with her days and evenings. She is trying to eat pudding with a crushed banana, or a magic cup or apple sauce. It is more and more difficult for her to swallow. Medications are administered sublingually. I looked into her eyes and felt two things that I have never been able to before. First, she told me that she was tired and secondly, that she was struggling. She stared at me as tears flowed out of her eyes. I have never, ever felt so close to her in my life. This was a special moment. I knew that Sarah was losing her battle. She was telling me in no uncertain terms that she was giving up her fight.

December 2008 –Sarah rests peacefully without food or drink. Her breathing is more and more strained and difficult. She is on oxygen, but appears to turn blue at times. I don't know how much longer she can continue this way. I don't know how much longer I will be able to watch this. I never pictured it ending this way. I'm not strong enough to face it. No words will describe my feelings and emotions. Sarah is one hell of a fighter.

December 5, 2008 – Sarah was pronounced dead at 5:00pm. She is at peace and in heaven. She has been freed forever from the demon called Alzheimer's.

LESSONS LEARNED

FORMULA FOR SUCCESS

Diet
Exercise
Monitor health and personality
Encourage faith and self-esteem
Natural sleep
Talk to confident, clergy, elder attorney, physician, family, support group, or diary
Include daily doses of humor and fun
Avoid negativism

Chapter 8
WHERE WAS GOD?

I asked Sarah if she was mad and she said, "Yes." I asked her who she was mad at and she said, "God." (4/26/07)

The most frequent questions that I was asked while Sarah was sick were – 1. "Where was God while this was happening? 2. How could God let this happen? 3. Why did God abandon you during Sarah's illness? 4. Where was God when the suffering was going on? 5. Why didn't God lift a finger to help or lessen your burden? 6. Why did this happen to Sarah at such a young age? 7. How did you survive so many years?"

I thought these were more than fair and reasonable questions, since I had asked them of myself at one time or another, but I couldn't answer them. Alzheimer's definitely tests and can even destroy the willingness and ability to pray. It makes you vulnerable to the point that it can eliminate your faith and trust in God.

Care partners will likely experience a spiritual crisis as they go through the five stages of development. I was on the brink of losing my faith and the ability to pray. I was desperate because God was ignoring us and our prayers. I doubted His existence. I didn't get what I wanted when I wanted it; therefore, my prayers fell on deaf ears. I knew God had abandoned us. I was not given solutions to the dilemma that I was facing. The bottom line was simple—why continue to waste my time and effort praying and believing in God, if it didn't help us?

Being the devious person that I was, I decided that God would expect me to get angry and stop praying and practicing my faith. I'm not sure if it was the severe stress or the hopelessness, but I did just the opposite. I continued to go to church and pray on a regular basis because I thought that was the right thing to do.

That bizarre behavior prompted me to think long and hard and to make up my mind if there could be a spiritual side implied in Alzheimer's disease. I know that during this long period of turmoil I prayed daily for any help, which was normal. We tend to resort to prayer during any crisis. I begged God to change our fate, but my prayers fell on deaf ears because Sarah continued to progress. Again, I was convinced that God abandoned us. Sarah would still be alive and at my side, if He had only listened to me and taken more of an interest. He could have saved Sarah, or so I thought. That statement might seem a harsh, but it has plagued me since Sarah's death. Reflecting throughout the grief cycle has helped me to recognize and understand that there is a spiritual feature associated with this disease. Investigating, finding, understanding and admitting that connection is an individual experience, but that I will tell you about my efforts and findings.

It was a long project. I have learned and admitted, only after Sarah's death, that God did not abandon us, as I initially perceived. He was with us all the time, but as with many of life's trials and tribulations, I could not grasp and admit that, especially in the midst of a crisis. I believe and now affirm that my survival was only made possible by an unlimited supply of faith and love with truckloads of patience and humor. That survival was what allowed Sarah's extended life and my experience of survival to tell this story to others.

As I think about faith and the spiritual aspects of the identity thief, a legend about the rite of passage for Cherokee Indian boys comes to mind. This tale suggests that a Cherokee youngster is taken out into the woods by his father. He is blindfolded and told to sit alone on a tree stump for the entire night. He is not permitted to cry out for help or remove his blindfold until daybreak. If he survives the entire night alone, he is considered to have reached his manhood. The youth is not permitted to tell any other boys about his experience because it is something that they must all experience on their own, in order to achieve manhood. It is a terrifying night for a young boy as he hears the wind blow along with all types of strange and unusual animal and other noises. In this case, the Indian boy sat as calmly as possible, until the sun appeared and he removed his blindfold. It was at then that he realized that his father had been sitting on the stump next to him for the night to protect him from harm.

Sarah and I were not alone during the last twenty-one years. God was sitting on a tree stump next to us. He watched over us while Sarah journeyed through the stages of her Alzheimer's and I progressed through the care-partner milestones. Unfortunately, care-partners are so overburdened, that they are often not capable of opening their hearts and minds to God's presence. This is true even when He is helping them.

Let me explore that concept a little further. I have always loved to skip rocks in the calm waters of a lake or river. I have looked at rocks that had been submerged in the water for years and often wondered if they were dry or wet in the center. Curiosity got the best of me. I cut several larger rocks in half to look at their centers. In every case, I found it to be completely dry. Evidently, rocks have a protective shield around them that prevents water from reaching their center.

The same principle applies to spirituality for care-partners. Care-partners develop a strong protective shield around them, especially after years in that role. That shield prevents anything from penetrating their center or heart. It even prevents God from getting in there. Care-partners wear blinders that prevent them from seeing or acknowledging that He is sitting on a tree stump next to them during their time of need because their outer layer prevents God's presence from penetrating their defenses.

I am no different than the average care-partner. I have no special powers or gifts. Religion is not a topic that I feel comfortable discussing or defending. I have always been a practicing Catholic and as such have attended church on a regular basis. I try my best to take an active role in the church and its teachings. As you have already seen, I too progressed through the five care-partner milestones just like everyone else normally does. I developed a strong and overpowering personality complete with its accompanying protective shields. I was blinded to the presence and possible intervention of God. Alzheimer's actually tested my faith daily; however, in the end, it strengthened rather than destroyed my faith and religious beliefs through a deeper appreciation and acceptance of God's presence.

I espouse that my twenty-one year survival was the result of a combination of faith and love coupled with an overabundance of patience and humor. Sarah was also a role model throughout her illness, as a woman, mother, grandmother and teacher. Without those attributes (faith, love, patience and humor – which was God's message.) and Sarah as my role model, I would never have made it as far as I have, nor would I have reached my goal as a survivor. As with many care-partners, it was not until after Sarah's death that I was in a better position and state of mind to be able to grasp that God was sitting on a tree stump next to me offering His support and a helping hand. I will demonstrate how this happened by describing a number of episodes that Sarah and I experienced over the years.

The first spiritual encounter was subtle and started out as a habit for Sarah. She wore an angel pin on her clothing dating back to the early years of our marriage. That habit continued and was a thorn in my side for her years in the early and middle stages. Sarah misplaced or lost an angel pin every day and I was tasked with finding or replacing it. I will never understand how Sarah remembered that she wanted to wear an angel pin daily after she had lost both her short and long term memory. She could not remember where she was going or what she was doing, but she never forgot that she wanted to look for and put on her angel pin each and every morning. I learned quickly to collect a supply of angels to avoid a crisis situation. I was a hero whenever I found or replaced a missing angel. They must have been her strength and inspiration day because she could not function without wearing one. It must have been God's way of reminding us that He was there and watching over us. He was sitting on that tree stump next to Sarah reassuring her that He was taking every step of her journey with her into her unknown and scary world. He wanted her to know that He would was always there.

Sarah showed several other signs of her inner strength and faith. We always went to church together. During the last four years that Sarah was home, I put Sarah into a wheelchair when we went to church. That made it much easier to keep her at my side. It also had a calming effect on her. I made arrangements with an usher before mass to have the priest bring the Eucharist to her in the rear of the church, instead of her going up to the altar. That was the best and most discrete way because Sarah was self-conscious about her condition. She believed that people were staring at her, especially when I pushed her to the altar in her wheelchair.

Receiving the Eucharist on Sunday's was special to Sarah. That prompted me to bring Communion to her every Sunday, once she moved into at a long-term care facility. I was amazed that I always had her undivided attention when we prayed together. That convinced me that she understood and processed everything that was happening. She was calm and reverent. She did not say the prayers with me, but she did move her lips, as if she were mouthing the words. I felt special and was honored to have been able to do that until two weeks before she died.

Sarah showed the same reverence when our pastor came to the nursing home during her last year, to administer the anointing of the sick. He also gave her Communion. I was concerned that she was going to pass out during her final anointing. I attributed that to the fact that she understood the reason for the blessing and more importantly, that she was on a downhill slide and probably going to die soon. God was sitting on that tree stump next to her, watching over and comforting her.

The second spiritual encounter involved the long period of time that Sarah struggled with Alzheimer's. She was fortunate to have taken at least one of the Alzheimer's medications for eleven years. I feel it is more than coincidence that she took two of the newest medications before they were available to the general public. It makes me wonder if her medications could have helped to prolong her life. I have found no research to validate that theory, but it makes sense. The medications combined with the special care that God permitted me to give her may have added years to her life. God was sitting on a tree stump next to us helping Sarah to educate others, and me, about this horrendous disease. He also gave me the gift of additional time with my lover, spouse and best friend. Of course, I did not consciously recognize that at that time because of the protective shield that surrounded me in the form of my special personality. I cherish and am extremely thankful for the extra quality time that I was given with Sarah. My only regret is that it ended so prematurely.

The third spiritual encounter highlights Sarah's positive attitude from the time of her diagnosis until her death. She taught all of us to live life to its fullest. She made it known that she experienced heaven on earth before and during her illness. She was eager to arrive at her permanent room in the heavens with God, but only after her work on this earth was done. She showed a strong desire to help others affected by this disease. In spite of the stress associated with such a diagnosis, she stayed positive and kept a smile on her face. Her laughter helped us to remain upbeat.

Sarah stayed positive even after she had lost most of her ability to communicate. I asked Sarah the same question every day when I visited her in the nursing home—Are you happy? She always said, "Happy." On an exceptionally good day, Sarah would say, "happy, happy." That was followed with eye contact that acknowledged her feelings. It made me feel so happy to see that Sarah was able to understand me and trying to communicate in her own special way. On one occasion, I saw that Sarah was sad and out of sorts. When I asked her if she was happy, she responded with a loud 'raspberry.' I laughed because Sarah was telling me in her own way that she was not feeling well and that she did not want to be bothered. That prompted me to relax and quietly support her. I held her hand and walked with her in silence, which kept her happy and content. My presence gave her reassurance that I was there to love and support her.

Sarah communicated with me in special and unique ways, and when I least expected it. It took a great deal of time, understanding, patience and effort on my part to capture and appreciate those important encounters. These quotes from Sarah should help you to appreciate how alert and savvy Sarah was mentally especially during the last year, when she appeared to be lost in her own world. God was showing me daily that she was there with me although she was not always able to communicate with words.

Sarah's Special Quotes

3/3/05—Sarah sat on my lap and said. "This is nice."

3/23/05—Sarah looked into my eyes and said, "I love you."

5/8/05—Sarah reached her hands out to me and said, "Hello."

5/14/05—Sarah said, "I missed you."

7/8/05—I asked Sarah, "Do you know my name?" She said, "No, but I like you."

8/1/05—Sarah reached with her hands and said, "Ah, Ah, I love you."

9/25/05—Sarah said, "I love you. You are wonderful."

1/26/07—Sarah's nurse asked Sarah where I was prior to my arrival. Sarah said, "He's home."

4/26/07—She was upset and anxious. I asked her if she was mad. She said, "Yes." I asked who she was mad at. She said, "God."

1/16/08—Sarah was passing out and said, "It's happening," as she went unconscious.

7/21/08—Sarah was sitting in her wheelchair. She yelled, "I won't go."

I could fill pages with Sarah's quotes particularly when apparently in the stages of Alzheimer's disease to emphasize her awareness and presence of mind. It took time and patience to wait for and capture these special moments. Some family members, friends and professional caregivers never reach the point that they are able to seize these times. Sarah wanted desperately to communicate and she did. It is another example of God sitting on a tree stump next to her and helping me to better understand her passion to communicate and remain close to me.

Sarah made one other special comment three years before she died. I purposely separated this from the other examples because it had such a tremendous impact on me. I attended a funeral mass for a member of one of my support groups who died from Alzheimer's. I was impressed with the priest's homily during her mass. He had a lot of experience working with dementia patients during his career. He suggested that they were talking to God when they appeared oblivious to the world around them. He said that they might be talking about us, but that was none of our business. I didn't think any more about that homily until several weeks later on July 1, 2005. I was walking with Sarah when she was confused and anxious. She was a million miles away and in a trance. I asked her whether she was thinking or talking to someone. She did not respond or look at me. I asked her again, if she was talking to someone. She said, "Yes." I asked her who she was talking to and she said, "God." Once again, He was sitting on a tree stump next to Sarah talking to and supporting her. I am convinced that she was talking to God and it was none of my business what they were talking about.

Sarah showed a positive attitude throughout her illness. She was my role model. She motivated both of us to wage a fierce battle against Alzheimer's disease. We worked with the local chapter of the Alzheimer's Association. She felt a special bond by sharing those feelings and emotions with others at a support group who had received a similar diagnosis. Whenever I asked her to make a presentation, she would always say, "Yes, if it will help someone else out."

Sarah's positive attitude encouraged us to be enthusiastic participants in one of the first support groups in the Tidewater area of Virginia for people with Alzheimer's and their care-partners. It was a new concept at that time. There were numerous support groups for care-partners, but there were none for the victims of the disease itself. Sarah told me often how important that group was to her. She was close to the members of the group because they understood what she was going through. She also believed that, she reached out and helped other members in her group, who were struggling. That support group gave

Sarah so much understanding that no one else, including me was able to give her. It helped her to cope with the changes that she faced. That encouraged me to form a similar support group in Richmond. I still help to facilitate that group which was formed during 2000. What a tribute to Sarah's memory. I believe that Sarah's positive attitude, desire to share her story and to help others, and her participation in support groups were another example of God sitting on the tree stump next to us.

The next involves one of the most important and delicate areas for most of care-partners. It came to my attention that Sarah had gotten lost on several occasions while she was driving to or from work or our daughter's house. It happened more than I realized because Sarah was very skilled at covering up that she had gotten lost. I wanted to ignore it because it was unpleasant to address. I considered taking Sarah's driver's license away to be yet another spiritual experience. Stopping victims of dementia from driving can be one of the most delicate, difficult and distasteful actions that a care-partner will have to take in his/her career. It involves the loss of a rite of passage, freedom and independence. It is something that most people have done since high school. It is often the biggest source of tension between a care-partner and their loved.

My background wouldn't let me ignore Sarah's driving difficulties. We discussed her getting lost. She admitted that driving was a scary challenge. After a long talk, I asked Sarah to stop driving. Much to my surprise, she rolled over and agreed to stop driving. There was no argument. She was relived because driving terrified her, but she was not sure what she should do about it.

Sarah surrendered her license in 1993 at the same time that she voluntarily retired from her job as a Medical Assistant. I was surprised that she agreed so quickly and easily to stop working and driving. I believe that she was relieved in both instances. She was happy to give them up because they were a chore and sense of embarrassment. She could not remember to think, react and handle things the way that she had done in the past. Sarah never showed an interest in driving or having her license after that. This was yet another example of God sitting on a tree stump next to us looking out not only for Sarah's safety and well-being, but also that of the citizens of the Commonwealth of Virginia. He answered my prayers and lightened my burden, although I did not recognize or appreciate it at that time.

The next happened during Sarah's middle stage when I was immersed in the frenzy phase. My stress level was well beyond my tolerance limits, but I was convinced that I could wage a successful battle against the identity thief by myself. I did not want any help. I was obsessed with the idea that I could find the magic formula that would enable me to do this forever.

I gravitated toward the use of alcohol. I drank a few more beers every night hoping to make myself forget and relax. I knew that it was wrong, but I continued to follow that same destructive pattern. At that same time, I could feel myself becoming increasingly more frustrated, annoyed and short with Sarah and her disease. I did not stop drinking because I felt that I needed it because the world closing in on me. I was falling apart at the seams. I, of all people should have known better.

I never gave up praying throughout this pattern of self-destruction, although it didn't seem to do any good. I still cannot fully understand or explain why, but one day I decided to change my ways. I would never have been able to do that without God's guidance and support. I stopped drinking cold turkey because I wanted to. I never looked or reverted back. I did not need alcohol as a crutch because it didn't solve any of my problems. God was discretely answering my prayers and producing miracles when and where I least expected them.

The next occurred when those disturbing, dark and distressing thoughts ruled my mind. I uncovered a number of different ways that I could free Sarah and me from the grasp of her Alzheimer's. I thought initially about poisoning Sarah. That would be quick and hopefully painless. I knew it was wrong, but Sarah would be free of her demon. Actually, it would do two things. It would free Sarah and it would also prevent me from having to break my promise. I was obsessed with this thought because I wanted out so badly. I would not be able to live with myself if I did anything like that, but it made sense at the time.

I never did anything to hurt Sarah, although those ideas haunted me from time to time. It became increasingly more difficult to sit back and do nothing as I watched Sarah disappear.

I latched onto a new idea. I decided to kill myself. I believe that I was close to following through on that. I starred at my weapon nights trying to get up the nerve to do something. I loaded and unloaded it. I practiced putting it to my head and in my mouth hoping that it would discharge by accident. I thought about playing Russian roulette. I was sure that I was going insane.

I decided that I couldn't kill myself and leave Sarah behind. I then thought about killing Sarah and then killing myself. By doing that, there would be no more suffering. No more worries about the progression and who would take care of Sarah if something happened to me.

I thought about doing it early in the morning on a secluded section of the oceanfront in Virginia Beach. We loved the ocean, so what better place to end it all? I wanted so desperately end to this nightmare. I was sure that I could carry out my plans.

Gradually, my thoughts gravitated to my upbringing, my career, my beliefs and morals, our family meeting, our children, grandchildren and God. How could I do something like that? It went against everything and anything that I ever learned or believed in. Would God forgive me? It would have a devastating effect on our kids and grandkids. What a horrible legacy to leave them. No one deserved that. I was confused. I wanted to make sense out of these evil thoughts because they were so disruptive and annoying. I wanted to face them head on without looking for the easy way out, but my mind was clouded by the stress, exhaustion and confusion. I wanted to rule suicide out, but I couldn't get it out of my mind. I am not an expert on the topic of suicide, but I felt that I was close. God was working overtime. He made sure that I ignored the easy way out in favor of sorting things out and facing the unknown. I feel that my struggles were miracles that had been occurring throughout my long ordeal without my ever acknowledging them.

I prayed hard to God for a resolution to my liking, but nothing happened quickly. I felt that God abandoned us again. I was helpless, alone and depressed. Somehow, I was given the strength to schedule an appointment to talk to a psychologist to help me to sort things out. I listened to what I had preached for years during my stress lectures when I told students that a healthy person seeks help. That is precisely what I did. To this day, I cannot believe that I did it. Counseling was not my first choice to solve any problem. I have never shared my feelings or emotions with anyone other than Sarah. That was definitely God answering my prayers.

My first visit to the psychologist was a disaster. My emotions spiraled out of control. I could barely talk to him at all. As luck would have it, I only needed to attend a few counseling sessions. I recall the psychologist saying during my last visit, "I guess you are not ready to let Sarah go." My first reaction to that was, 'Bingo,' finally someone knows where I am. I felt that he knew what he was talking about. He finally said, "You will know when it is time." I felt good at least for the moment. I believed inwardly that I would never be able to or have to, let Sarah go.

I left the psychologists office feeling that the weight of the world had been removed from my shoulders. I had a new sense of dedication, strength and energy. I was convinced that I would be able to take care of Sarah till the end; however, as you will see, that didn't last for long. Again, God was working behind the scenes to protect us both.

I have never talked about this next spiritual encounter. I feared that people would think that I was crazy, if I told them about it. It was the early part of 2003, a month before Sarah's gall bladder surgery. Somehow she contracted the noro-virus. It was a horrible experience because of my weaknesses. I avoided changing diapers when our children were infants. Whenever I had to, I sprayed perfume or something sweet smelling to mask any odor. That stopped me from gagging and getting sick. It was something that I dreaded and despised because it was so embarrassing. Sarah was the opposite. She could do anything.

The noro-virus was like nothing I have ever experienced. Sarah vomited and had diarrhea without interruption for twenty-four hours. I was at my wits end and had lost track of time. I changed Sarah's pajamas and the bedding and showered her three times during the night. The bedroom and bathroom were a mess. I finished changing, cleaning and dressing Sarah. I'd put her back to bed and the cycle started again. I didn't have time enough to wash bedclothes or bedding and I was running out of both. I was in a state of total panic! I had never felt so sick, weak, and disgusted in my life. I cried while I was cleaning the bathroom and shower. I didn't feel as if I had an ounce of strength to continue. I had had it! I reached the end of my rope and it was only 3:00 am. I needed help, but there was no one and nothing available. I couldn't stop gagging. I was sick to my stomach. All of a sudden, I felt a warm, gentle hand on my shoulder. I was afraid to turn around because I knew that there was no one else in the house. The touch of that hand radiated strength, confidence and calmness throughout my body. It might sound crazy, but I honestly and truly had the sensation of a hand on my shoulder. I can't explain it, but it was a life changing moment. I am convinced that God used that sensation to bring me back to reality and restore my confidence.

All of my weaknesses, despair, feelings of abandonment, and panic disappeared. I worked for the remainder of that night without any problem. I did it all. Nothing bothered or frustrated me. As the evening went on, I suspected that Sarah was dehydrated, so I transported her to the emergency room where they confirmed that she had the noro-virus. I brought her home that afternoon, because God had been watching over and protecting us.

Two weeks later, a similar scenario materialized, when Sarah had a severe attack of pancreatitis. I did what I needed to do once again without any problem to get us through the night. Sarah passed out in the shower at 5:00 am. I had her transported to the emergency room for treatment. That second evening, I was still awestruck by the memory of that previous evening. I was amazed at my performance. I am convinced that I would never have been able to get through either night without that exceptional experience. It reminded that God is and has always been there, but I failed to see or acknowledge His presence.

On the afternoon of January 25, 2005, I was involved in yet another episode. I was driving home from my visit to Sarah. It was not the normal and uneventful drive because I was in the middle of a severe and treacherous ice storm. There is no way that I should have been on the road, but I would not skip my visit to Sarah. I drove forty-two of the forty-five miles without any problem. There were wrecks everywhere, but I avoided any problems. I was on the road leading to my subdivision. I was over-confident that I would get home safely. I drove a little faster than I should have for the worsening ice conditions. I came to the crest of a hill and found that that road was closed because of wrecks. I locked my brakes and spun around once heading toward the wrecks. What a helpless and sick feeling as I waited to hit the cars in front of me. I kept turning the steering wheel like crazy to gain control or change my direction, but a wreck seemed inevitable. I slid to the left instead of into the stopped cars. I came to rest in the parking lot of a church without hitting anything. I didn't hit a curb or any islands. I couldn't believe what had just happened. There was no way that I could have ever avoided hitting those cars. I said a prayer of thanksgiving because it was nothing short of a miracle. God was sitting on a tree stump and protecting me from myself and the elements that day.

The next and most extraordinary encounter began on August 5, 2007 when Sarah was enrolled in a new hospice program. It ended at 5:00 pm on Friday, December 5, 2008, when Sarah died. During that entire time, Kelly M. Nixon, RN was her nurse. For that year and a half, Ms. Nixon tirelessly focused on Sarah's comfort, dignity and a pain-free environment. She assured me that Sarah's physical, emotional and spiritual needs were also being met. Ms. Nixon was miraculously present at the time of Sarah's death. I could not have planned it any better in a million years. Arline Bohannon, MD, Virginia Commonwealth University Health System (Sarah's physician) also made frequent and odd hour visits to coordinate with Kelly and oversee Sarah's care, comfort, and dignity in her declining weeks and days. I continued to see God sitting on the tree stump next to us making sure everything went well for Sarah and apparently just as Sarah and He had preplanned together during one of their many conversations.

I forwarded the following letter to the Chief Executive Officer of Ms. Nixon's hospice group to express our appreciation for the awesome way that she cared for Sarah. I would like to share that letter which reinforces just how much of a spiritual encounter that aspect of Sarah's care actually was for the Schaefer family:

Dear ...:
Sarah P. Schaefer, my wife, was admitted into your hospice program on 8/30/07, as a victim of Alzheimer's disease. She remained in hospice for an unusually long period of time, but not without valid reasons. It was the opinion of her doctor at the time of her admission that Sarah would quickly succumb to the pneumonia that seemed to be getting the best of her. Well, she fooled all of us when she survived the

pneumonia; however, she continued to decline and weaken significantly from the ravages of her Alzheimer's.

Sarah's progression was unique and unlike many other dementia patients. She continued to be plagued with seizures, tremors and all kinds of unexplained neurological changes. Her decline was extremely slow, painful, and difficult to witness. I know that because I visited her daily, to offer what support and comfort I could. At the time of her death, Sarah had lost all of her activities of daily living and any of those functions, pleasures, and senses that we all tend to take for granted. Sarah died due to complications from her Alzheimer's disease at 5:00 pm on Friday, 12/5/08. I was present at the time of her death and I am so thankful that Sarah was under hospice care, to enable her to pass away with peace, dignity, and compassion. It was extremely difficult to be with her at the end, but Ms. Kelly M. Nixon, RN, her Hospice Nurse helped us all to better understand what was occurring and why.

We were so blessed, fortunate and privileged to have been associated with your hospice team. (In that team, I include Kelly M. Nixon as Sarah's RN, Grace as her Certified Nursing Assistant. Those were the individuals that we had the most frequent contact with during the past year and a half.) I know that I speak for my entire family when I say that Kelly M. Nixon, RN, was an 'Angel sent from God'. We truly believe that. What an asset she is to your organization. She made a difference in all of our lives and the way that we responded to this horrific loss. I do not know how we would have survived without Ms. Nixon accompanying us on our journey as she displayed daily doses of love, peace, patience, goodness, faithfulness, and gentleness, all of which help us to accept the inevitable. The care and support that she was able to offer us all will never be forgotten. We were so fortunate to have had Ms. Nixon at Sarah's bedside as she passed away. What a special gift and comfort to us all. She truly is an 'Angel sent from God.'

Please take the time to thank and commend Ms. Nixon personally for us for her time, effort and dedication, which was above and beyond the call of duty. She did an awesome job! Additionally, I've noticed on my daily visits that this was not only true for Sarah, but all of the patients that Ms. Nixon worked with at Lucy Corr Village. She is an extremely unique and talented individual and as I previously mentioned is a tremendous asset to your organization.

I have attached a donation, which I wish could have been more. I give this in honor of Kelly M. Nixon, RN, for her service and dedication to her patients who are facing their biggest and most frightening challenges ever. They are all so fortunate to have met a 'Special Angel of God' on this earth.

Sincerely,

Robert B. Schaefer

The next spiritual encounter had to do with the tremendous and continuous source of strength that I received from my family, friends, and other organizations. I was gifted to have the support and encouragement of our four children and their spouses and our eleven grandchildren. Several long-time and special friends and couples visited us whenever possible. They also called me on a regular basis for the entire twenty-one years, to offer their prayers and support. Additionally, I consistently received support and advice from the Greater Richmond and the Southeastern, Virginia Chapters of the Alzheimer's Association. Sarah was so blessed during the last four years of her life to have been under the care of the outstanding professional caregivers in the Clover Hill Neighborhood at Lucy Corr Village and for her last two and a half years to have been enrolled in hospice, which I think is the most underutilized program available to the victims of Alzheimer's. That phenomenal support made life so much easier and more bearable for the both of us and all of our family. I am convinced that this was another fine example of the spiritual link that can exist when God sits next to us during our times of crisis.

I saved one final and powerful spiritual lesson and as my final example. I am sure that Sarah wanted to better prepare me for the inevitable – her death! She was determined to die gracefully and without fear. I will never forget when Sarah told me at 5:00 pm on November 11, 2008 that she was dying. I reached over and held her hand. It was at that point that I did the hardest thing that I have ever been called upon to do. I gave Sarah permission to die. It was probably the third time that I had done that for her. It did not make it any easier for me knowing that I had done it before. In fact, it seemed to be more and more difficult every time that I was called upon to do it. I told her everything was okay and she didn't have to worry. I said that the children will be okay. We are all taken care of. I will be okay. You are in God's hands now. You do what He wants you to do. We are all so proud of you. Please, close your eyes and relax. You deserve to be at peace. Sarah quickly drifted back off to sleep. Twenty-five days later almost to the minute, she died. I know that she did so on her own terms. Our children had either visited their Mom on the day that she died or were returning to visit her because they knew that the end was near. Jane, her sister and I were the only ones at her bedside when she died. That was exactly the way that I had hoped and prayed that it would happen. I know that that was also Sarah's wish.

LESSONS LEARNED

• When we share what we have with those who are in need, we too, will discover God in our midst.

• Miracles happen when we least expect them.

• God is always with us, He is not 'out there.'

Chapter 9
A NEW CHAPTER

Today was the first anniversary of Sarah's death.

As usual, I was at the fitness room at 5:00 am for my daily workout. Somehow, today was different. I couldn't work out. Nothing felt right so I returned home to sit in my recliner. I was not able to do anything else. I sensed that I was regressing back to a year ago when I pulled a security blanket over my head and hid from everyone and everything.

I remained motionless in my recliner for several hours until I went to mass for Sarah's anniversary. I drove to the cemetery after church and placed artificial poinsettias at Sarah's marker for the holidays.

It was very chilly and raining hard, but I stood in the weather for a few minutes to fuss at God and Sarah because I was not happy that she had been taken away from me. I felt better for the moment.

I went home to my recliner and held on tightly to that security blanket.

Every bit of feeling and emotion was slowly drained out

of my body over the next eight hours. As I think about it, God brought me to a major turning point in my life and the grief cycle. He channeled every bit of the anger, bitterness, depression, and negativism out of my body, so that I could begin anew. He listened to my prayers and wanted me make the best of what I had. The rest was up to me. He was telling me not to try to understand all that had happened, but to move on and continue to do His will, whatever that might be. I feel confident that I will be a survivor and enjoy my new life as long as I follow the guidance offered by God and Sarah, as I explore the unknown. (12/5/09)

My life changed profoundly when I lost Sarah on Friday, December 5, 2008. On that day, I began one of the most challenging and painful passages of my life. I had twenty-one long years to prepare for this inevitable event, yet I found that I was ill-prepared when it arrived. I do not think that I will ever be able to put into words what went through my mind and happened physically, mentally and emotionally, as I watched every last bit of life taken from Sarah. Her life was extinguished breath by breath during those last weeks, days, hours, minutes and seconds. It was not what I wanted or expected to happen. It was much worse than I ever could have imagined! I have talked to other care-partners who have lost their loved ones and their reactions were unmistakably similar.

My toughest and most painful challenge was to let Sarah go. That was a tall order. It baffles me because I have studied the grieving process and served as a facilitator for such a support group. My journey has been much more difficult than I ever could have imagined. I am aware of what has happened, but cannot absorb and digest what I need to do to continue on this extraordinary journey. I read an awesome poem by Edgar Albert Guest (1851 – 1959). This insightful poem accurately puts into words what I should be doing, to pull through this treacherous path of my life. His words require no comment or clarification.

MISS ME BUT LET ME GO

When I come to the end of the road and the sun has set for me.
I want no rites in a gloom filled room, why cry for a soul set free?
Miss me a little…but not too long, and not with your head bowed low.
Remember the love that was once shared, miss me…but let me go.

For this is a journey we all must take and each must go alone.
It's all part of the Master's plan, a step on the road to home.
When you are lonely and sick of heart go to the friends we know,
And bury your sorrows in doing good deeds.
Miss Me…But Let me Go.

Sarah's death brought me to a new time and place. I am not sure if I will ever find my way back to any type of regularity. Letting go has been hampered by the void that I experience on a daily basis. I'm not sure that will ever leave me. Sarah and I were one in the true sense of the word after we were married, bound, unified and joined. Now, I am one, but the meaning has changed to single and solitary, which translates into alone. One is so lonely. It tugs and will continue to tug at my heartstrings.

Part of my reluctance to let go is undoubtedly due to the reality that Sarah was special to me. That was true from the moment we met. She was my world. Perhaps this chapter will ease the ache and help me take the necessary baby steps that will ease my mending.

Sarah was my best friend, lover and confidant. She was the only human being that has ever been in touch with my feelings and emotions. That was so true after she tricked me into going to a Marriage Encounter Weekend. As a typical male, I resisted that with all of my might; however, it was the best and most positive thing that we did as a couple. We grew tremendously in the years following that experience. Communication improved to the point that we experienced a unique happiness that we could never have attained without that resource. Sarah was the only person to whom I have ever told my true feelings and emotions without reservation because that weekend changed my perceptions. It was crystal clear that I could trust her. I loved Sarah more than anything else on this earth.

Sarah fought with every bit of her strength, spirit, and energy right up to her last breath because she did not want to leave me alone. She was not willing to let go easily. She was a true and gallant fighter. I felt helpless and useless watching her lose her battle because I had no control over her horrendous disease. It was painful to do nothing, except hold her hand and smile. I wanted to run away and not return, but I would not let myself break a second promise to Sarah by letting her die alone. I could not have done that and lived with the guilt.

I was blessed that our children spent time with their mother during her final hours. I am thankful that they were spared seeing her take her last breath, as I did. Jane and I watched together the last day as Sarah struggled with every breath to fight her destiny. I can still hear her blurting out to God months prior, "I won't go." As I watched Sarah struggle, I said a prayer of thanksgiving for the opportunity, honor and privilege to be with Sarah to the moment that God took her home. My biggest fear has always been that I would die first or she would die when I was not with her. I didn't want her to die alone. I wanted to hold her hand as she journeyed into the unknown. That thought caused many a sleepless night over the last twenty-one years.

It was and is still difficult to believe that Sarah died. It was not real at the time. I rehearsed that moment for years, but denial kept me believing that it would ever happen. I did not want to let Sarah go without a fight. How could I ever walk away from her? I did not know how to do that. This is all so confusing. I am puzzled, but I suspect confusion is all part of the grieving process.

I have no idea what my family or I would have done or how we would have reacted, if Kelly M. Nixon had not been there from hospice. Ms. Nixon prevented us from falling apart. She was there daily for the last two years taking care of Sarah's special and unique needs. Miraculously, she was at Sarah's side during her last few hours, minutes and seconds. She watched Sarah take her last breath with Jane and me. It couldn't have been planned any better. Ms. Nixon shined that last day of Sarah's life, as she professionally and skillfully guided our family through the events leading up to Sarah's death. Kelly was the best and excelled at what she did. She performed her duties with an awesome air of professionalism, expertise, and confidence. She made sure that Sarah maintained her dignity and was comfortable and without any pain. We all felt that Ms. Nixon made it possible for Sarah to leave Lucy Corr Village with the peace, pride and dignity that she deserved. She was an angel sent to us by God. What an awesome testimonial Ms. Nixon was to the hospice.

I cannot say enough about the Procession of Honor that took place after Sarah's death. It was a relatively new ceremony available to families of residents who passed away at Lucy Corr. It should definitely become a tradition that is never eliminated. Members of our family, a few select friends and available members of the nursing staff proudly surrounded Sarah's body as we walked her through the halls of Lucy Corr toward the main entrance. Sarah was draped in a special quilt, while her all-time favorite hymn, Amazing Grace, was played in the background. She left Lucy Corr with the pride and dignity that she deserved and through the same front door that she had entered four years earlier. The emotion generated by everyone went beyond mortal words and description. I will always remember that procession and how proud Sarah must have been as she departed this earth for her heavenly reward.

Before I leave the subject of Lucy Corr, I have nothing but high praise and heartfelt thanks for the nursing staff and the care they provided Sarah for the four plus years that she lived there. Their care was special to Sarah and to the Schaefer family. It was a special gift and a bit of heaven for Sarah, while she was still here on earth.

I thank and commend Tyler Harrell, RN, Neighborhood Care Manager and Ms. Cynthia Simms, LPN – Charge Nurse in the Clover Hill Neighborhood. Without their presence, supervision, counseling, dedication, and expertise, none of this would have been a reality.

I would be remiss if I did not single out two special CNAs who took care of Sarah on a regular basis and for the longest time that she was in the Clover Hill. I acknowledge, thank, commend, and praise Bertha Hall, CNA, who I affectionately referred to as 'Sarah's room mother.' Bertha took care of Sarah days for her entire stay at Clover Hill. I have never met a finer, more caring and loving person. I always felt comfortable missing an occasional visit, if I knew that Bertha was on duty and taking care of Sarah. I knew that she was in good hands. She changed my mind, which is not an easy task. I realized that there were others in the world of long-term care that could and would take care of Sarah in the same way that I took care of her while she was at home. Bertha cared for and loved Sarah as if she were a member of her family. I can say the same for Gwendolyn Lauderdale, CNA, who took care of Sarah on the evening shift, but for a shorter period of time. I must also thank Latrella Burnett, CNA, who cared for Sarah on the midnight shift and was additionally responsible for bathing her. I acknowledge and thank Anastasia Chiwengo, CNA, who took care of Sarah frequently, but mostly on weekends, especially during her last few months in the Clover Hill Neighborhood.

Sarah was always treated so very special by the LPNs who were the first to respond to her falls, episodes of syncope, seizures and of course medications. I acknowledge and thank Carrie Salomone, who I affectionately call Florence. Carrie drew on her previous experience as a hair stylist and volunteered to cut Sarah's hair once it became apparent that she could no longer go to the beauty salon there. An otherwise unbearable and unpleasant task was made so much easier for

Sarah and me. She was special to have done that. I thank Sarah Jones, LPN, who worked more hours in Clover Hill Neighborhood than any other member of the nursing staff. LPNs Ola and Utari had less contact with Sarah, but nonetheless went out of their way to make her comfortable and pain free, especially during her last few weeks.

Thank you to the following individuals, who were all very special and kind especially during Sarah's last few months in the Clover Hill Neighborhood: Beverly, Elia, Irene, Joyce, Kristan, Regina and Zinda. My biggest fear is that I have unintentionally omitted someone's name that was deserving of recognition. If I have, I apologize. I also thank housekeepers Dottie and Joyce for their dedication and understanding, especially during Sarah's last few months in the unit.

I barely remember driving home alone, which was my choice that night. I was in a state of shock and disbelief and should not have been driving, but I felt a strong, compulsion to be alone. It was a combination of my law enforcement and care-partner personalities shinning and protecting me. I didn't want to show any feelings or emotions. I forced myself to think that it was a bad dream and I would wake up and Sarah would be on the road to recovery. I felt I was losing control of my mind and my body. I kept seeing Sarah take her last breath. That image haunted me. This was scary for me because I wanted, and more importantly needed, to be in control of my feelings and emotions. I started to sob, but I fought like crazy to hold it in because that did not fit my image. I wouldn't be caught dead sobbing or crying about anything.

I drove home slowly because I felt my emotions taking over. No matter how hard I wished and tried I was not able to stop the emotion from flowing. I don't remember that happening to me before. Tears began to flow and before I knew it I was crying my eyes out. I could barely see the road through the tears. I had to stop on the shoulder a couple times to regain my composure and dry my eyes. I drove slowly because I didn't want to be stopped by a trooper. I couldn't bear the thought of anyone seeing me like that. I feared I would not be able to talk if I were stopped. I thought that surely a trooper would think that I was a slobbering drunk and take me to jail.

I arrived to a house full of family. I wanted to mingle and talk, but I was not able to control my emotions. My stay with them was short-lived. News about Sarah's death spread like wildfire and the telephone began ringing. I went into my office, shut the door and sat in the darkness. That generated strength enough for me to regain some control of my emotions – or so I thought. That did not happen for a time. I could not answer or make telephone calls. Thank God my sons, Sean and Bobby sensed that and made appropriate notifications and answered incoming calls. I could not talk to anyone in person or on the phone for that night and days.

I had to be alone. It was a strange, strong and compelling feeling. I didn't want to see or talk to anyone – not even family. I couldn't do it. I wanted to shut everyone and everything out. I hurt badly, but I didn't know what I should or could do. I had no control over my mind and my body. I did not know how to handle the pain because it was so consuming.

Our kids rallied to ensure that I maintained my space for that first evening and the days that followed. I sat in the darkness of my office crying in disbelief at what had happened. I wanted to go back to Lucy Corr and have it happen again with a different ending. I kept flashing back to Sarah's face and her last breaths. They will be etched in my mind for ever. My sobbing turned into crying and finally into whaling. I didn't think that I would ever be able to stop and I really didn't care.

I knew that I couldn't face anyone in that condition because I as a man, police officer, FBI agent and care-partner had been programmed not to show emotion. It was a sign of weakness and failure. Damn manhood, the macho image, and the law enforcement and care-partner personalities. They made the grieving process more difficult. I kept thinking that I was dreaming. I wanted to go to sleep, wake up and visit Sarah so that everything would be back to normal. Unfortunately, sleep was out of the question. My situation was not changing no matter how hard I wished for a more pleasant ending.

I did not sleep that first night. I dozed for a half hour or so in my recliner. My mind was spinning. I was in a non-stop mode of thinking 'what if.' Had I been too aggressive with Sarah's medications and treatments over those last months, weeks or days? Should I have been more patient? Should I have done things differently? If I had, would my Sarah still be alive? I felt horrible guilt. Did I cause Sarah to die when and how she did? I wanted to blame myself.

Those bizarre thoughts did not let me to sleep or eat for weeks. I spent nights in my recliner or on the couch trying to get a few hours sleep. Every time that my eyes closed, I flashed back to Sarah's last breaths and that was the end on my sleep. I second guessed myself for hours. I relived Sarah's last days trying to find out where I had gone wrong. Those disturbing thoughts resulted in hours of crying, the likes of which, I had never experienced. Crying filled days and nights. I didn't think that I would ever stop. Anything and everything caused me to lose it and I did not know what to do. I didn't want to go anyplace or do anything. I was content to sit day and night in the dark with a blanket over my head. I couldn't listen to the radio or watch television without something being said that reminded of Sarah. I wanted her back badly, but there was nothing that I could do, and I wasn't willing to accept that.

After a year, I realize that I have been wasting my time questioning what I could have done better. I have been stuck in the past. That means that I have not let go and accepted Sarah's loss. I am trying to grasp the notion that it is time to move on with my life rather than trying to understand or change what has happened. I am trying to refocus on what is, but that is a tall order. It will take time, effort and energy to make that a reality. I must let go completely in order to proceed with my new life.

The only regret that I have was not taking a few minutes to be alone with Sarah right after she died. Ms. Nixon asked me if I wanted to spend any time alone with her before the funeral director arrived. Without thinking, I told her that I did not. I had just spent the last month or better, day and night at Sarah's beside. I was with her when she died. Why would I need to be alone with her again? Now, I wish that I had gone back and shared a few extra precious minutes to talk and pray with her. I was in shock and denial and didn't realize the finality of what had just happened. I did not realize that Sarah would be transported to the University of Virginia Health Center for a diagnostic brain autopsy and I would never see Sarah again. For some reason, that did not sink in until it was too late.

Final arrangements were made over the next few days for Sarah's services. I am thankful that I listened to the advice of the Alzheimer's Association, hospice and other care-partners who suggested that I complete the necessary arrangements in advance of her death. Fortunately, I wrote her obituary several months before I needed it. I realize that I would never have been able to do that in the emotional state that I was during those first few days. I could only answer questions with a yes or a no. There was no other conversation. I went to the funeral home and the church with my sons. I signed paper after paper fighting off the tears that continued to get the best of me. When this was done, I returned to the darkness of my office. I needed that security blanket over my head so that I could escape.

We met with family members and friends an hour before Sarah's funeral mass in a reception room at St. John Neumann Catholic Church in Powhatan, Virginia. A fellow instructor of mine, Miles Turner, prepared a wonderful slide presentation that pictures Sarah from birth to death. Everyone marveled because it was such a beautiful tribute to Sarah, her personality, love and zest for life. Many were amazed to see themselves in photographs with Sarah from years past.

The dreaded moment arrived when we were ushered into the church for the mass. Everything was hazy, because I was in a trance. I held up emotionally, while we greeted family and friends, but reality caught up with me at the mass. Father Jeffrey Garcia officiated at the mass. His homily was beautiful and an outstanding tribute to Sarah and her family.

Jane did the first reading, Sean the second and Bobby read the Prayers of the Faithful. Rosemary Harper, Sean and Bobby represented the Family in the Final Commendation and Farewell. Sean read a beautiful and moving letter that his daughter Megan wrote to Sarah in heaven after she died. There wasn't a dry eye in the church. I prepared a Final Tribute to Sarah, which I wanted to read. I was too distraught so I asked my nephew, Stephen Schaefer from Miami to read it. Steve did an awesome job. His delivery was superb to the point that everyone thought that he had written it. I was so happy and proud that I had asked Steve. Sarah must have been grinning from ear to ear. Here is my tribute:

MY TRIBUTE TO SARAH

I cannot let this opportunity pass without saying a few words – because that is what Sarah would have expected of me.

"How do I love thee? Let me count the ways. I love thee to the depth and breadth and height my soul can reach…"

That is the first line of Sarah's all-time favorite poem by Elizabeth Barrett Browning. Sarah recited it while we were dating and after we were married. I tried to ignore her because I thought it was too mushy for me. She gave the poem to me on a large index card that she typed on her office typewriter if you still remember what that is. I carried the original index card for forty-three years in my datebook.

Those of you who know me well would never believe that I was the shyest man on this earth when I met Sarah. It was Sarah and her unending love and devotion that brought me out of my shell and made me the successful, loving, caring, giving, and sensitive person that I am today. She taught me the important things about life up to her last breath Friday evening.

I was so shy that even after our marriage, I rarely shared my private thoughts, feelings and emotions with Sarah and that drove her crazy. Her favorite question became, "Honey, what are you thinking about?" My initial answer was always nothing. Sarah's persistence along with a Marriage Encounter weekend changed that. I must say that that was one of the most positive, powerful, and important changes in my life. Sarah read me like a book and was the only human being that could penetrate the protective shield that shielded me in the form of the law enforcement personality.

Before I leave shyness, I must relate one story that occurred during our courtship. We met in April and were married in December. A short time before our wedding, Monsignor Philbin or Father Bill, Sarah's uncle was representing her dad, who had passed away. Father Bill was also marrying us. One evening, Father Bill told me that he would meet with me in the basement of her home. Sarah was not aware that any of this was taking place. With Sarah's mother, Frances, listening at the top of the stairs, Father Bill told me that he would not permit this wedding to happen because our courtship had been too short and we really didn't know each other well enough. Father Bill said that the marriage would not work. I don't think that it is necessary to get specific about our conversation, but I was agitated as I spoke up and defended our relationship and impending marriage. I noticed that Father Bill could not hold in the laughter and Frances almost fell down the stairs laughing, as he revealed that it was a joke. They wanted to see if I would speak up for Sarah and show my love because I was so shy and quiet. None of those antics made Sarah happy. I hope that the last forty-three years have left no doubt about my love and devotion for Sarah.

Sarah was not a fashion plate and did not compete with the Jones', but she did have a thing for shoes and purses. Unfortunately, she lost most of the purses during the progression of her Alzheimer's. Sarah was only interested in raising her children to be caring, loving, sensitive, and generous. Sarah, as I look at Tom, Sean, Bobby and Kathy and their families – I see that you did an awesome job. There is so much of you in your children and that radiates from them, especially since you have left us. I only wish that Sarah could have had more time with her grandchildren because she loved and adored them. One other example of Sarah's giving and thinking of others occurred when we lived in Northern Virginia and I was in the FBIs Behavioral Science Unit at the FBI Academy. Sarah voluntarily gave up a full day with Tom, Sean, and Bobby when they went with me to sit at the bedside of a young FBI agent at the hospital. He had been shot in a gun battle with a fugitive. It didn't matter to Sarah that it was Christmas Day that she let us go – it only mattered to her that this agent was taken care of, or otherwise he would have spent Christmas day alone without anyone to visit and cheer him up.

It is a little known fact that I had a goal of having fifteen children. I proved it by putting it on my license plate in New York after we were married. The tag read—RBS-15. When people asked what that meant, I told them that that was the number of children that we wanted to have. Sarah was surprised, but remained silent. The doctor's foiled our plans after eight pregnancies, which included four miscarriages, because it was too risky for her to get pregnant again. Her hair stopped graying at that point. We were part of a study made up of only three families in the US who had four children, to include three boys and one girl who all had pyloric stenosis. We were told that we could make medical history by having a set of twins that had the same disorder. Of course, that could not happen now.

Sarah taught me that it is not the personal possessions, but the legacy that you leave behind when you die. Wow, Sarah, what a legacy you left. Sarah and I always joked about seeing a u-haul in a funeral possession to carry treasures. Sarah doesn't need a u-haul for her personal possessions because she leaves behind a legacy of her children and grandchildren, love, faith, sensitivity, caring, giving – and I could go on forever. Sarah's faith lasted to her final week. I brought her Communion each and every Sunday for the five years that she was in a nursing facility. She always showed some recognition that she was about to pray and receive "The Body of Christ."

I am thankful that Sarah chose me as her husband. I was told that Sarah would marry a man in uniform. It was a contest between myself in my New York State Police uniform and a gentleman named Sid in his Navy uniform from the Naval Academy at Annapolis. I remember a story about Sarah having Sid at the back door, while I was at the front door to take her out on a date. It was a better rivalry than the Army – Navy game, but in this case the State Police triumphed.

Sarah was the boss throughout our years together and I'm proud of that. She exerting her authority during our first year of marriage when I signed up to attend motorcycle school in the State Police, which had been always been a dream. She was vehemently opposed because of the danger. I remember clearly leaving for my first day at cycle school. Sarah kissed me good bye and said in a very clear and soft voice, "If you go to cycle school today, I will not be here when you get home tonight". Needless to say, I resigned from the school because I was not willing to see if Sarah would follow through on her promise.

Sarah was a teacher and pathfinder in the early onset of Alzheimer's for twenty-one years, whether she knew it or not. She participated in one of the first support groups in the Tidewater area of Virginia for the early onset victims of Alzheimer's and their care-partners. She motivated me to start another such group when we relocated to the Richmond area. That group started around 2000 is still in existence.

Sarah talked to others about Alzheimer's, especially newly diagnosed patients. She told them how it felt to receive a diagnosis of the 'probable early onset of Alzheimer's disease". This was part of Sarah's continuing legacy of teaching, giving and, helping others.

The closing words of Sarah's favorite poem – How Do I Love Thee? is perfect here:

"…I love thee with the breath, smiles, tears and all of life! And if God choose, I shall love thee better after death."

Sarah I love and miss you so much – I feel like my heart, soul and very being have left with you – God speed!

The mass ended and we made the long journey to the Veteran's Cemetery in Amelia, Virginia, where Sarah's ashes were buried. Following a short prayer service, final blessings and goodbyes in the Cemetery Chapel, we returned home. We were not permitted to visit the graveside immediately following internment.

Our children planned a reception for family members and friends at a model house in my development. I was well into my own world, trance, stupor, or whatever it is called. It was not like anything that I felt before. I didn't really care about anything, but I had to make an appearance and try to go with the flow until our guests left.

I had the intense and unending compulsion to be alone. I hid myself in the darkness and put that security blanket over my head to shut everyone out. That became an integral part of my coping. I didn't know how to deal with what was and had happened to me. I did not want to learn or be told by anyone how I should help myself.

I followed that pattern for weeks. A very special person helped to guide me through the dreaded Christmas holiday. I will not identify that person who is or was not looking for any recognition or thanks. They took time away from their family and friends to accompany me to the cemetery on Christmas Day, after making sure that I ate a delicious, wholesome and nutritious breakfast. I dreaded visiting because I knew it would be difficult and emotional. I was exhausted and didn't know how I could generate any further emotion, but I did. I am so grateful for the special love, caring, support and that person, who convinced me to do away with my security blanket and start facing reality. I believe that is part of the reason that I am here today and completing this book.

Several weeks after Sarah died I stopped my volunteer work, training and support groups in the Alzheimer's arena. I put it all behind me and tried to start anew. I wanted to sell my house, buy a motor home and travel nowhere for the rest of my life. I had a strong desire to get away from everything that was familiar. I wanted to do something drastic, but I wasn't sure what that was. I wanted to feel better. I thought that moving to Florida, which was always a dream of Sarah's and mine would make me forget and it would help to heal my wounds. Believe it or not, those dark thoughts that plagued me earlier returned. I could not bear to be without Sarah. Suicide again seemed like the route to take to solve my problems. I thought about going into the seminary to become a priest. What a contrast – I was so torn. I knew one thing. I wanted to feel better. I was getting more depressed as the hours passed. I was hurting, but I couldn't help myself.

I did one impulsive thing a few weeks after Sarah's death with the hope of making myself feel better. I spent weeks looking for a new car which I didn't need. It diverted my attention and gave me something to do and prevented me from thinking about what I had experienced. Kathy and Scott looked with me. I did buy a car, but it did not help my grieving. Nothing changed psychologically and emotionally and I was saddled with a new payment book.

I caution anyone who has experienced the loss of a spouse to resist doing anything impulsive involving large sums of money that you might regret, at least during the first year of grieving. You might feel better for a moment or two, but when the evenings approach, it will not lessen the loneliness and emotions that have entered into your life.

I completed several bereavement courses and seminars in the past. I helped to start a bereavement ministry at my church. Two things jumped out during those trainings. The first was to give time—time. The second was not to make major decisions, especially if they involved large sums of money. This is definitely true for at least the first year. I did put all of my thoughts about moving, motor homes and the priesthood on the back burner. I did stop volunteer work with the Alzheimer's for several months. I am gradually moving back into that arena.

The grieving process has been difficult. I understand some of this has been my own doing. I do not want be unhappy or torture myself, but that is what I am doing. I am at a loss as to how I can change my focus even after a year has passed. I hate to say it again, but I am struggling in part because of my background. I have spent a lifetime not showing feelings or emotions to anyone outside of my circle, under any circumstances. I am a problem solver. Since Sarah is gone, I do not have, and probably will never have, a confidant. That does not help my feelings of inadequacy, loneliness and confusion.

In the days and weeks following Sarah's death, I visited her grave every day. I thought that I would be abandoning her if I didn't. I needed to be with her just like at Lucy Corr. I suspect that was my guilt coming out. I had such a routine that it was a way of life. It was my job. I was supposed to do it. All of a sudden, I was in so confused; I was not able to visit any longer and I did not want to give that up. I needed it. I prayed harder than I have ever for help and guidance. Slowly, I began to accept that I was not in control. It was not a dream or a fantasy – it was reality. My behavior was counterproductive and I needed to change. If I didn't change, I would remain stuck in the past.

There was a bright-spot on December 13, 2008 when the Schaefer family and a few select friends went to the Clover Hill Neighborhood to present a Christmas concert in Sarah'sMemory.

After a year of moving in slow motion, letting go is still a challenge and stumbling block. I attended a weekday mass recently. Father Jeff's homily hit between the eyes. It was as if he sensed that I was stuck. He talked directly to me that day. He discussed a spouse losing a partner after years of marriage. Spouses can develop a mindset that they cannot continue with their lives because of their loss. Life no longer has meaning. He said that way of thinking was wrong and counterproductive. It should be avoided. He pointed out that you survived before your spouse ever came along and you married; consequently, you can survive when your spouse dies. It is more appropriate to focus on the fact that God left you on this earth for a purpose. You might not know or understand what it is, so pray for guidance with a clear, positive and productive attitude. It may become clear in time as you live your new life. He speculated that some might be left behind to be with and help their families, children or grandchildren. Still others to complete worthy charitable work, while some might be destined to help someone in a way that you never thought or anticipated. It may be possible to develop another relationship that will further enrich your life further. He suggested frequent prayer, a positive attitude and a goal of victory. Try to avoid negativism and a loss of faith during your period of mourning.

I thought long and hard about Father Jeff's homily. I have experienced extreme lows, but no happiness. I have decided that I am not entitled to enjoy myself, which is in direct conflict with his homily. I have been negative, but I have not been strong enough to change my attitude and perceptions. My brain blocks positive thoughts from coming into my mind. It stops fun and laughter. In fact, I do not think that I am capable of laughing or having fun anymore. I want to be positive and see the brighter side, but I'm being held back. I am responsible for my attitude, but at times, I feel helpless.

I have seen myself going through stages similar to those of a care-partner. I have experienced denial, resentment and anger, and an alteration of personality. I have a new identity. I have been immersed in the frenzy stage; I have not yet reached the tolerance milestone. I continue to pray for strength and guidance during this period of turmoil.

I monitor my behavior, attitudes, and perceptions and my extreme lows. I visit my physician on a regular basis. I have been offered, but refused sleep aids or anti-depressants. I continue to exercise regularly. In fact, I have expanded that to include several aerobic activities with the hope of accelerating my healing process. It has been a long, slow, tedious, and exhausting process, but I am determined to accept and excel in my new life regardless of how long that transition might take.

Evenings and sleeping are challenges. Loneliness rears its ugly head every evening. I'm not sure that it will ever go away. My hope is that the intensity will lessen in time. I have lost interest in television, news, and sports. Nothing appeals to me anymore. I sit and struggle as my mind is bombarded with thoughts and memories from the past. That makes me more lonely and depressed. My emotional outbursts have lessened considerably, but still visit me more than I would like.

I try to go to sleep as early as 8:00 pm because I don't want to be alone. I begin my night's sleep in a recliner or on the couch. If I go directly into bed, I toss and turn with aches and pains until I get up. I don't know if this is related to the years of sleeping with one eye open, while I was taking care of Sarah waiting for odd hour calls from the nursing home. It might also be missing Sarah in the bed, which always bothered me. I find that hard to believe because I have not slept next to Sarah for years. In fact, I have a new bed that Sarah has never even seen. I am confident that time will help to overcome these oddities.

I was relieved, revitalized and inspired by reviewing the University of Virginia Health System Autopsy Neuro Procedure Report resulting from Sarah's diagnostic brain autopsy. It read, in part: "Together with clinical history, examination of the gross and microscopic material demonstrated the presence of a primary neurological disease with all the features of advanced Alzheimer's disease. Numerous amyloid plaques and neurofibrillary tangles were identified...Given the patient's age, frequency and distribution of plaques, the appropriate CERAD stage is 'C,' which represents a definite (versus possible or probable) diagnosis of Alzheimer's disease. Tangles were identified in the hippocampus, inferior parietal cortex, superior temporal gyrus and occipital cortex, yielding a Braak and Braak topographical stage VI/VI (the most progressed stage in the B&B system.)..."

There is one aspect of this report that disturbs me. There is a possibility that Sarah had the familial type of early onset, since I have learned that Sarah's uncle was diagnosed with 'senility,' while he was in his fifties. If that is the case, our children could be at a higher risk of being diagnosed with Alzheimer's disease.

There is no doubt that Sarah was taken from me by Alzheimer's disease, which is the identity thief of the 21st Century. The diagnosis is comforting in one sense because my volunteer hours were well spent in the Alzheimer's arena. That has inspired and given me a fresh outlook for the future. I will continue as a helper and share the valuable knowledge and experience that Sarah has given to me. I am sure that God left me on this earth to wage a fierce war against Alzheimer's. I returned as a facilitator and co-facilitator for my support groups. I with two others have started and facilitated a bereavement support group for the families of the victims of Alzheimer's disease in the Richmond area. I volunteer, speak, and train for the Alzheimer's Association. I returned to my First Responder Training at the Department of Criminal Justice Services. I serve as a Commissioner on the Governor's Commission for Alzheimer's and Related Disorders. The only activity that I have stopped, at least for the present time, is volunteering as an Ombudsman for the Health Center and Assisted Living Community at Lucy Corr Village. I am distancing myself from Lucy Corr, at least for the time being, until I feel that I have made it
through the grieving process.

Writing this last chapter has provoked me to wonder what advice Sarah would give me if she were able to talk to me today—one year after her death. I have been considering taking ten days away from my routine and volunteering, to visit my sister and brother at a time—share in Coco Beach, Florida. I would love to go, but something is holding me back – it is that feeling that I am not supposed to laugh or have fun.

I visualize Sarah saying the following: "Honey, I love and miss you very much. You are having a difficult time letting go and moving on with your life. You deserve better than that. First and foremost, listen to the advice that you have given to others during your stress lectures and support group meetings. You have been good at helping others go through periods of crisis, but now that you are experiencing a crisis of your own, you are putting blinders on and doing the direct opposite of what you teach others to do. You are stuck in yesterday, which I've heard you repeatedly say to others. That will destroy you. Listen to me when I tell that you must change your mind, attitude and perception about your new life.

You are letting the grieving process get the best of you and that is a not good. It hurts and you want to avoid more pain and discomfort. You need to face it – you can handle it. I have faith in you. You cannot run away or hide, which is exactly what you are trying to do. You are letting image armor hide and protect you from what you need to face head on. You recognize that better than anyone else, but you are ignoring the obvious. Break through that image armor and stop hiding in the darkness of your office because that will not help you. Do not be afraid of your emotions. You learned and practiced that so well when you were with me. Continue to do that so that I can be proud of you.

Remember, you taught me to laugh and be positive when I thought that my world was about to come to an end. Well, what about you – I don't hear any laughing. Your attitude is negative. It is okay to let your hair down and have fun. I expect nothing less from you, but you won't let it happen. Stop punishing yourself. You were a wonderful husband and an awesome care-partner. You did what you had to do and you were the best at it. Don't feel the least bit guilty about placing me in a facility or letting me go. I begged you with my eyes for years to do that very thing, but your guilt prevented you from seeing it. I could not have asked for any more. It is time for you to recover and to accept your rewards, which will undoubtedly involve well-deserved peace and happiness. Shake it off and get into that new car of yours and drive to Florida. Give my regards to Jackie and Norbert and have fun talking about the good old days. Think and laugh about the days that we shared together. Spend a night at St. Augustine Beach for old times' sake and think about the many times that we visited and had so much fun there.

I do not think that your involvement in the Alzheimer's arena is bad. In fact, a lot of people will benefit from you having walked the walk. You have so much knowledge and experience to share. You can help people in a way that no one else is or has been able to do. Keep up the good work, but don't be totally consumed with it. Take off those blinders and stop punishing yourself.

Put time and effort into enjoying yourself. I know that you gave up everything that was near and dear to you during the twenty-one years that you took care of me. You always put my needs before yours. Please recognize your tunnel vision. Regroup and try to focus on something that will help you to move on and through this difficult passage. God has given you extra precious time on earth for a reason. Do not waste it. He wants you to help others, but He also wants you to live your life to the fullest without feeling guilty, grieving and being stuck in the past. You will never forget and stop loving me, but it is time for you to begin enjoying your new life. It is time for Bob to take care of Bob. I have always worried about what would happen to you if I died first. I even picked out a couple perspective new wives for you because I did not want you to be alone. Well, I'm not saying that you have to run out and get married, but there are some special people out there that might need you and you might need them. You will never find a special person to love, help and support and let them love, help and support you, until this passage is complete. Your work is cut out for you. Move out of your world of sorrow and despair and start to live. Please do not disappoint me. I will be watching. God is sitting on that tree stump next to you and I will be with Him, whenever He permits, to offer you support and guidance.

Please finish your book. I expect you to put an autographed copy in the bookcase in my honor. I am excited about it and the love, passion, time, effort, and emotion that you have put into it. Always remember that you can do it if you try – I will be waiting for you to complete your tasks on earth. I love you!"

My response to Sarah is – "Sarah, I know in my heart that I must let go. I love you with all of my heart and my soul. I will never ever forget you, but I believe that it is time for me to bid you a final and fond farewell. I need to do that so that you can be about your heavenly business without worrying about me, as I hopefully with your blessing work my way successfully through this process and return my life to some type of normality with a new identity, goals, objectives and challenges. At that time, and prompted by your memory and personal guidance, I will be able to complete that unfinished business for which God has left me on earth. "

I will end this chapter by offering 'advice and food for thought' to family members and friends who have offered a wide variety of suggestions and advice to hasten my progression through the grieving process. Hopefully, this will be of value to all who face a loss in the future.

I believe that the grieving process involving Alzheimer's disease is different than the victims of other diseases. This is due to the fierceness of Alzheimer's and the long and slow progression that often destroys personalities and identities. The loss of a spouse is more traumatic and emotional than the loss of a grandparent, parent, sibling, other family member or friend. I am not demeaning these other losses, but the loss of a spouse tends to generate more havoc for survivors than any other relationship.

All too often people place time limits on the grief process. This is dictated by the norms of our here and now society. It can also be caused by people feeling uneasy and not understanding the grief cycle, especially when someone is overwhelmed or stuck longer than they should be. The words in the following poem offer guidance for this natural process. It is awesome and appropriately demonstrates my feelings and emotions over this last year.

Don't tell me that you understand,
Don't tell me that you know.
Don't tell me that I will survive,
How I will surely grow.

Don't tell me this is just a test,
That I am truly blessed.
That I am chosen for this task,
Apart from all the rest.

Don't come at me with answers
That can only come from me.
Don't tell me how my grief will pass
That I will soon be free.

Don't stand in pious judgment
Of the bonds I must untie,
Don't tell me how to suffer,
And don't tell me how to cry.

My life is filled with selfishness,
My pain is all I see.
But I need you, I need your love,
Unconditionally.

Accept me in my ups and downs,
I need someone to share.
Just hold my hand and let me cry
And say, "My friend, I care."
(By Joenetta Hendel)

LESSONS LEARNED

- "Leap and the net will appear" (John Burroughs)

- "Miss Me, But Let Me go"

- Live life to the fullest because it ain't worth saving

- "You may be only one person in the world, but you may be the world to one person." (Author Unknown)